THE PRACTICE OF PERFECTION

ALSO BY ROBERT AITKEN

Encouraging Words

The Dragon Who Never Sleeps

The Gateless Barrier

The Mind of Clover

Taking the Path of Zen

A Zen Wave

The Ground We Share
(with David Steindl-Rast)

THE PRACTICE OF PERFECTION

The Pāramitās from a Zen Buddhist Perspective

Robert Aitken

PANTHEON BOOKS NEW YORK AND SAN FRANCISCO

 Published in the United States by Pantheon Books, a division of Random House, Inc., New York, and simultaneously in Canada by Random House of Canada Limited, Toronto.

The essays in this book were published in an earlier form in *Mind Moon Circle.*
The first chapter appeared in an earlier form in *Turning Wheel* and *Mountain Record.*

The circle calligraphy by Suzuki Shunryū Rōshi is reproduced by permission of the San Francisco Zen Center.

Library of Congress Cataloging-in-Publication Data

Aitken, Robert, 1917–
The practice of perfection : the Pāramitās from a Zen Buddhist perspective / Robert Aitken.
p. cm.
ISBN 0-679-43510-7
1. Pāramitās (Buddhism) 2. Zen Buddhism—Ethics, Doctrines. I. Title.
BQ4336.A37 1994
294.3′444—dc20 93-47095 CIP

Book design by Maura Fadden Rosenthal

Manufactured in the United States of America
First Edition
2 4 6 8 9 7 5 3 1

To the compassionate presence of
Nyogen Senzaki

CONTENTS

ACKNOWLEDGMENTS

This book evolved from classes at Diamond Sangha centers and from talks at institutes of the Buddhist Peace Fellowship, and at seminars at Goat-in-the-Road and in the Department of Religion, University of Hawai'i. I am grateful to many people who assisted with preparations. Transcriptions were made by Susan Garfield and a number of helpers at the Koko An Zendō. Laurie and Alan Senauke and Jason Binford brought coherence and order to the question-and-response sections. Anne Aitken and Jason Binford gave careful study to preliminary drafts and made valuable editorial suggestions. Finally, I want to thank my editor, Jack Shoemaker of Pantheon Books, who knows what I want to say and makes me say it.

INTRODUCTION

The Pāramitās, or Perfections, evolved with the advent of Mahāyāna Buddhism some two thousand years ago. They were derived from the three-part teaching of Classical Buddhism: Shīla, Samādhi, and Prajñā—morality, absorption, and wisdom.[1] They also derived from the love of categories and classifications that distinguishes the culture of India. Though at first these lists can seem tedious, with unpacking they produce the treasures I seek to burnish in this book.

The first four Pāramitās relate to morality: Dāna, giving; Shīla, the moral code; Kshānti, forbearance; and Vīrya, vitality or zeal. The fifth Pāramitā is Dhyāna, *zazen* (settled, focused meditation)—a term and practice closely related to Samādhi. The sixth is Prajñā itself, or wisdom.

Like other Buddhist teachings, the Pāramitās unfolded with experimentation over time. After the first six were established in the first few centuries of the Mahāyāna, the decimal system of arithmetic was invented and many of the categories and formulas of Yoga and Buddhism were rounded off to ten. It seems possible that for this reason four more Pāramitās were added to the original six: Upāya, compassionate means; Pranidhāna, aspiration; Bala, spiritual strength; and Jñāna, knowledge.

It is also possible that the evolution of Ten Pāramitās in Theravāda commentaries (as a different set of Perfections) influenced the Mahāyāna teachers to increase their own table to ten, or that the Ten Stages of the Bodhisattva set forth in Mahāyāna literature established a precedent for an equivalent number of Pāramitās. In any case, we can be grateful for the inclusion of these additional Pāramitās. No matter what the reason for their inclusion, they clarify our way of practice and deepen our understanding.

The Pāramitās are inspirations, not fixed rules. We honor them with our conduct, speech, and thought. Shāntideva, the great seventh-century Buddhist teacher, cites with approval the wisdom of an early Mahāyāna sūtra: "The perfections of the Bodhisattva do not support me—it is I who support them."[2]

Though the Buddha Shākyamuni was transmuted with Anuttara-Samyaksambodhi, pure and complete wisdom and compassion, he nonetheless continues to support the Pāramitās. His work from the beginningless past through the endless future is to liberate himself and others. It is our work as well. Nobody, least of all the Buddha, can say, "I have accomplished it." Zazen is itself enlightenment—as Dōgen Kigen Zenji never tired of saying.[3] This means, in his words, that body and mind have dropped away and they continue to drop away endlessly. The self is forgotten and it continues to be forgotten more and more completely through all time.[4] Any residue of self-centered conduct, speech, or thought is wiped away. Any residue of that wiping away is then wiped away and so on endlessly—each day more liberated, each day more joyous. There are milestones on the path, as the Buddha found under the Bodhi tree, but they are no more than milestones and are not any kind of ultimate consummation. Perfection is a process.

ONE

GIVING

The Dāna Pāramitā

The dictionary definition of Dāna is charity or almsgiving—of goods, money, or the teaching. More generally, Dāna is the spirit and act of generosity. Its salutary effects are endless, and they multiply beyond measure at each point of renewal.

Thus, Dāna is intimately tied in with karma—cause and effect—while its neglect too has inevitable consequences. As Lewis Hyde says in his landmark book—*The Gift,* "When property is hoarded, thieves and beggars begin to be born to rich men's wives."[1]

It is with the Dāna Pāramitā that the Buddha's teaching of universal harmony is put into practice. Mutual interdependence becomes mutual intersupport. It is practice that is not only Buddhist but perennial as well. The Earth itself flourishes by what Emerson calls the endless circulation of the divine charity: "The wind sows the seed, the sun evaporates the sea, the wind blows the vapor to the field . . . the rain feeds the plant, the plant feeds the animal."[2] The very stars hold themselves on course through a mutual interchange of energy.

In keeping with this natural charity, ancient customs of gift giving and circulating the gift kept primal human society healthy. The Native Americans who greeted the Puritans in Massachusetts understood this well, though their guests, it seems, did not, for they scornfully called the customs "Indian giving." In its uncorrupted form, the potlatch ceremony of northwestern America was usually a grand ritual of giving away precious possessions by the tribe on the occasion of naming a new chief. Giving ennobles.[3] In dedicating our sūtras, we turn the virtue of the recitation back to Buddhas and Ancestral Teachers in gratitude for their guidance. We are constantly receiving that teaching, constantly sending it around again.

In Classical Buddhism there were several categories of Dāna. One category was dual, including both the pure charity that looks for no reward and the sullied "charity" whose object is personal benefit. Another formulation was triple: charity with goods, doctrine, and services. Other formulations make it clear that Dāna was traditionally considered to be preaching by monks, donations of clothing and medicine to the poor by temples, support of temples and monks by laypeople, and gifts to the poor by those laypeople who could afford them.

With the development of the Mahāyāna, the Sangha (kinship, fellowship) became universal, no longer centered upon monks and nuns and their temples. Dāna became the open door to realization, showing clearly what had been there from the beginning, for by any name and in any practice, Dāna is the hallmark of human maturity. The gift itself is food—often in fact, always by analogy. Its virtue is absorbed, renewed, and passed on to nurture all beings.

My teacher, Yamada Kōun Rōshi, used to say, "I wish to become like a great tree, shading all beings." The Dāna Pāramitā was his ideal, and I am grateful that he could put it into words so gracefully. Earlier Zen Buddhist expressions of Dāna are also heartening:

> *A monk asked Hui-hai, "By what means can the gateway of our school be entered?"*
>
> *Hui-hai said, "By means of the Dāna Pāramitā."*
>
> *The monk said, "According to the Buddha, the Bodhisattva Path comprises six Pāramitās. Why have you mentioned only the one? Please explain why this one alone provides a sufficient means for us to enter."*
>
> *Hui-hai said, "Deluded people fail to understand that the other five all proceed from the Dāna Pāramitā and that by its practice all the others are fulfilled."*

The monk asked, "Why is it called the Dāna Pāramitā?"
Hui-hai said, " 'Dāna' means 'relinquishment.' "
The monk asked, "Relinquishment of what?"
Hui-hai said, "Relinquishment of the dualism of opposites, which means relinquishment of ideas as to the dual nature of good and bad, being and non-being, void and non-void, pure and impure, and so on."[4]

Hui-hai does not include the dualism of self and other in his list of dichotomies we must relinquish, but it is clear that he intends that it be included, for he goes on to say, "By a single act of relinquishment, everything is relinquished. . . . I exhort you students to practice the way of relinquishment and nothing else, for it brings to perfection not only the other five Pāramitās but also myriads of other [practices]."[5]

This total relinquishment is the self forgotten, the dropped-away body and mind. It is still a center, but it is outflowing. The food and housing and clothing and money it requires to function are metabolized as giving—we eat to be able to serve, in other words. The ordinary way of receiving in order to receive even more becomes transformed into a way of sustaining the self in order to practice the Buddha's wisdom and compassion.

Yet "eating to serve" has a slightly righteous tone. If the self is outflowing, what is the stuff that flows out? Is it simply obligation? I hope not. Is it self-sacrifice? Perhaps it is, when viewed from outside. From a personal perspective, however, you will find that it is easier and more natural than the word *sacrifice* implies. Also, it is important to take care of the one who gives; otherwise, the flow dries up. Recreation, re-creation, is important for the Bodhisattva.

Finally, is it compassion? Yes, but a specific kind of compassion that arises with gratitude. The English word *gratitude* is related to *grace.* It is the enjoyment of receiving as expressed in giving. It is a living, vivid mirror in which giving and receiving form a dynamic practice of interaction. For receiving, too, is a practice. Look at the word *arigatō,* Japanese for "thank you." It means literally, "I have difficulty." In other words, "Your kindness makes it hard for me to respond with equal grace." Yet the practice of gift giving lies at the heart of Japanese culture. The word *arigatō* expresses the practice of receiving.

Dāna brightens and clarifies the Dharma, the Buddha Way, and with continued unfolding it brings natural authority for more brightening and clarifying. You see its power in those who are acknowledged as leaders in traditional societies. In American history, it is the authority of John Quincy Adams, who stepped down from the Office of President to serve selflessly in the House of Representatives for the last seventeen years of his long life. In Buddhist history, it is Tou-shuai relinquishing his role of master and returning to practice as a monk.[6] In relinquishing conventional power, Adams and Tou-shuai found the authority of the timeless. They pass it on to us, and with each gift of empowerment, the strength of Dāna in the world is enhanced. The Wheel of the Dharma turns accordingly.

Mu-chou, an elder brother of Lin-chi in the assembly of Huang-po, was a monk of great moral authority. In *The Blue Cliff Record,* he appears in an interesting story:

> *Mu-chou asked a monk, "Where have you just come from?" The monk gave a shout.*
>
> *Mu-chou said, "That's a shout on me." The monk shouted again.*
>
> *Mu-chou said, "Three shouts, four shouts, what then?" The monk said nothing.*
>
> *Mu-chou gave him a blow and said, "You thieving phony!"*[7]

At this time, Mu-chou lived quietly in a little hut near a highway where monks would call on him for instruction. When the monk in this story approached Mu-chou, he was undoubtedly psyched up for the occasion, ready for the deepest possible experience. It wasn't going to be an ordinary conversation at all. Mu-chou had a great reputation as a severe teacher. After all, it was he who broke Yün-men's leg in the course of enlightening him.[8]

So Mu-chou says, "Where have you just come from?"

The monk cries, "Khat!"

That first shout was pretty good. "Where do I come from? Come on!"—the monk seems to be saying—"Give me a break! That's really a smelly question."

"Oh," says Mu-chou gently, "you have shouted me down. You have beaten me at my own game. You are the sage and I am the ordinary fellow." You see Dāna functioning here. By temporizing, Mu-chou gives the monk free play. I can imagine how he fixed his eyes on the monk—can he step into the opening?

The monk shouted again. What do you make of that second shout? Mu-chou is disappointed and hardens his line just a little: "When you run out of shouts, what happens next?" There's another great chance, monk! I give you this space for a response. What do you say?

But he couldn't say anything. Stuck in the mud!—and Mu-chou gives his last great compassionate effort. *Whack!* "You faker!" There are many other examples of this kind of Dāna in Zen Buddhism. Lin-chi once shouted at a monk, "You shithead!"—or words to that effect.[9]

What happened to the monk when Mu-chou hit him and yelled insults at him? Nothing, probably. But it wasn't for want of Mu-chou's effort. In those sacred circumstances, where presumably the monk had mustered his body and mind in preparation for the deepest possible experience, Mu-chou was filling a Bodhisattva role as best he could, though he would have denied it such a label. His great concern for the monk extends to countless beings. Suppose you were that monk, sitting before Mu-chou. How would you respond to his question, "Three shouts, four shouts, what then?" Thus you can receive his Dāna as your own redemption. You can then take yourself in hand in similar situations and convey it to friends and family members.

Yet Mu-chou did not spend all his time in formal teaching. Between visitors, he occupied himself with making straw sandals of the kind worn by monks on pilgrimage. Such sandals are carefully crafted, but they wear out. So Mu-chou would weave them in various sizes and put them beside the highway. Monks would come along and say, "Oh, look at those nice sandals. I wonder where they came from? Let's see now, here's my size." And they would go on, with feelings of great gratitude. For a long time nobody knew who was making the sandals until finally Mu-chou was found out and became known as the "Sandal Monk."

Mu-chou practiced in his hut beside the road, teaching and crafting sandals—and we practice in our own circumstances. Dāna is simply remembering what we are, avatars of the Buddha, practicing our giving where we are. There is no need to call it Dāna Pāramitā. You and I are perfecting our outflowing selves, saving the many beings as we greet one another and encourage one another.

Dōgen Zenji said that giving a single phrase or verse of the teaching becomes a good seed in this life and other lives:

> *One should give even a single coin or a single blade of grass of resources—it causes roots of goodness in this age and other ages to sprout. Teaching too is treasure, material resources are teaching. It must depend on the will and aspiration.*

> *When one learns well, being born and dying are both giving. All productive labor is fundamentally giving. Entrusting flowers to the wind, birds to the season, also must be meritorious acts of giving. . . . It is not only a matter of exerting physical effort; one should not miss the right opportunity.*

> *Giving is to . . . transform the mind of living beings. . . . One should not calculate the greatness or smallness of the mind, nor the greatness or smallness of the thing. Nevertheless, there is a time when the mind transforms things, and there is giving in which things transform the mind.*[10]

Birth and death are both ultimate forms of giving, but the key to the practice of Dāna is Dōgen's observation that will and aspiration are its roots. Bodhichitta, the endeavor and hope for Buddhahood, is the fundamental motive. This is not merely endeavor and hope for personal realization. I return so often to the words of Hui-neng about the first of the "Great Vows for All," the Four Bodhisattva Vows: "The many beings are numberless; I vow to save them." This, Hui-neng said, is a matter of saving them in my own mind.[11] I vow to cultivate an attitude of saving, which is no other than the attitude of giving. This can be far more than charity. It can be the gift of body and mind, the experience of "Great Death" in Zen Buddhist terms.

Yet there is no need to wait for any kind of experience. You and I can practice the Dāna of trust and respect just as we are, *as if* it were perfected—and thus it is indeed perfected. With our own personalities and character traits, wearing our clothes and eating our meals, Shākyamuni and Kuan-yin practice "as if" we were Buddhas and Bodhisattvas, even in our smallest acts, catching the bus and answering the telephone. The will to practice is the only requisite.

QUESTIONS AND RESPONSES

Q. I wonder if you would say a little bit more about Dāna as relinquishment.

R. The implication of Dāna for laypeople in Classical Buddhism was that you give as you can afford to give. This is quite different from "dropping off body and mind."[12] In a very real sense we are practicing Dāna in our zazen, letting everything else go—all preconceptions and patterns that hold us together, all of what we must do in order to maintain what we are. Let go. Let go.

Now, there are natural limits to this. Forgetting the self does not mean getting rid of the self. You can't do that—you can't neglect who you are. Forgetting the self means forgetting "me" in zazen and in daily interaction, letting go of my preoccupations, and listening.

Can one practice body and mind falling away without letting go of all attachments? I have told the story of a woman who came from another state to study with us. She missed her books and was miserable, so I told her to send for them. I didn't presume to say, "You must give up your books." She would have to do that herself, if she needed to, which I don't think she did. Body and mind falling away is an experience of great emptiness. We come forth from there and read books.

Q. There's a tradition in Christianity and in Buddhism of giving everything away to follow the spirit. Could you talk about Dāna in that light?

R. Yes. I once saw a photograph of Gandhi's possessions. They fit into a small showcase. A copy of the *Bhagavad Gita,* a pair of eyeglasses, a dollar watch—such absolute necessities. The Buddhist monk or nun also has such a basic collection.

I'll tell you a story that a Canadian youth told us at the Maui Zendō many years ago. In Calcutta he had been robbed while he was asleep, so he had only his shorts. That's all. No shoes, no wallet, no passport, nothing. There was no Canadian consulate in Calcutta, so he went to the British consulate for help. They said, "You have to go to the Canadian embassy in Delhi." But then they reconsidered and told him to come back in a few days.

He had absolutely nothing. He wandered around and took shelter under a bridge. There he met some beggars. These beggars looked after him for the three or four days that he had to wait in order to get money and papers from the Canadian embassy in Delhi. It was a total revelation, a peak experience for him to realize that he didn't need anything—that he could trust in the world. But as he told the story, his new wallet was in his pocket and a new shirt was on his back.

Sometimes relinquishment can seem artificial. Fu Ta-shih, a contemporary of Bodhidharma and a lecturer to the emperor, took all his cash on a string and rowed out to the middle of the lake and dropped it in. People said, "Why didn't you give it to others?" He said, "Well, I didn't want to burden them with that problem." They said, "What about your family?" He said, "Well, they have to take care of themselves."

Looking at this from the perspective of modern Western culture, we might have lots of questions about Fu Ta-shih's action. But there are times—such as in a divorce, or on losing a job, or on being evicted—that one goes through a total giving up. It's a very important experience.

Q. What about the idea of relinquishing enlightenment? What does that taste like? What is the feeling of that relinquishing?

R. It's interesting. It's challenging. It's inspiring. You see, the Buddha did not stay under the Bodhi tree. He just sat there for a week after his great experience. Then he thought about his five former disciples stewing in Benares. He sought them out and gave his first sermon to them. For thirty-nine years thereafter he walked the dusty roads of the Ganges Valley preaching to large groups and conferring with individuals, turning the Wheel of the Dharma. He is our great teacher and we follow his way.

Q. In certain situations in life, I seem unable to let my heart open to certain people. That always troubles me because I think that if there is one person on the planet that I cannot open up to, then I can't really open to all the rest.

R. Don't be too hard on yourself. Join the club. Everybody has this problem. I remember hearing Thich Nhat Hanh speak about a very prominent person who had come to visit him. He said, "I can't relate to that person." If a saint like Thich Nhat Hanh can't relate to somebody . . . ?

It's a human failing. The fact that you recognize that you have this failing puts you squarely on the path to correcting it—squarely on the path to opening. How many people do you know who are so defensive they don't even think about opening themselves to others? There are lots of them. So be easy on yourself and acknowledge that you are having a hard time and that the Buddha himself had a hard time. Where you are, seek to open more, to ask, "What are you going through?"—even though you don't quite feel like asking it. Take that little step to open yourself to the other. That's practice. And remember that you yourself are one of those beings that you must be kind to.

Q. Does this relate to the idea that's really common in the helping professions, that if I give too much, I'll burn out? I've got to take care of myself in order to give?

R. You bet! That's a very important point. Yamada Rōshi said, "It's like pouring water in a bamboo basket." The teacher or the social worker or the librarian or the nurse or the doctor or anyone in a helping profession certainly needs a religion, in my view. One of the doctors I admire most, to whom I submitted my own body twice for operations, goes to Mass every morning of the world at six o'clock. Then he makes his rounds.

Q. I have problems with giving. My first impulse is to give everything, and then I get scared and think, "Oh, no, now I can't survive." I struggle with this a lot.

R. You and I are very much alike in this way. I understand your particular problem very well indeed, from a very personal point of view. I am constantly reminding myself that this pilgrim needs food and clothing and money and medicine and blankets and the rest of it. And a neat little laptop computer with which to write my stuff. If somebody were to come to me and say, "Give me your computer," I don't think I would be ready. But with most anything else, I would at least hesitate and think, "Well, maybe I don't need this." But I'm terrible about lending books, just terrible. They disappear and I think, "Where is that book? Who did I lend it to?"

It's your practice, really. It's your ongoing practice to take good care of yourself, because you yourself are the only one with your qualities in the whole world who has ever existed and who will ever exist again. You have a unique contribution to make and you need to nurture this one who is making that contribution.

Q. I hear you say that. But I get these guilt feelings.

R. Uh huh: "I didn't do enough."

Q. I didn't do enough or I'm taking too much time for myself. And so then you go back to the practice?

R. So then you practice—and you go to the movies. [Laughter] You need that stimulation; you need that recreation. You need to re-create this avatar. You need to take care of yourself. Otherwise, you can't function. You get too tired. You get too stressed.

Q. I'm on the Buddhist Peace Fellowship fund-raising committee, and I'm confused about the difference between giving people an opportunity for Dāna and soliciting for funds.

R. Well, we are told by professional fund-raisers that the spirit in which to ask for gifts is, "This is one option for you. This is one way for you to help to turn the Wheel." Not "We want this money," but "This is our program. If you like it, then we offer you the opportunity to help out."

Q. Would you like to be on the committee? [Laughter]

Now I have another question. Mu-chou whacked his student and called him a fake long ago, so I can understand his actions as Dāna. But if you were telling us that this happened yesterday in an American Buddhist community, I don't think I'd understand it as giving.

R. That's an important lesson in cultural diversity. You know, the verb that is used in Chinese as in English is *gave* him a whack. Our instruction in studying these kōans is that the final harsh words can be interpreted to mean: "You must take another step; please, go on." Really, there is something very pure about it. I've never whacked anybody in the dokusan room. Oh, occasionally someone will say, "Give me a tap with that stick." So I give a little tap. But it doesn't work.

Q. A few years ago in Sri Lanka, one of the world's poorest countries, people collected offerings to make a huge Buddha statue worth millions of dollars. They carried it across a lake on a boat and planned to install it on an island. Well, the boat sank because the statue was too heavy, and many people drowned. So I have questions about that.

R. Yes, I share your questions.

Q. But is there a way I can accept calamity as a teaching?

R. Accept it as best you can as part of your practice. "Maybe I can learn from this," you can say. "Maybe it will make me a better person, a Bodhisattva." I hope I can do that myself.

Q. While we're talking about perfectionism—I am living with someone who is very perfectionistic and who is very ascetic. I suspect that the asceticism comes from very deep feelings of unworthiness, and yet there is this ideal of asceticism and a simple life in Zen. I wonder if you would have anything to say about the possibility of helping someone else see their own perfection beyond their perfectionism?

R. Let me share a story about my teacher Yamada Rōshi. Have I told this before? If so, maybe it will be pertinent again. At one time we were sharing students: I was teaching in his absence, and then he would come and lead sesshin (the Zen Buddhist retreat). In speaking about one of the students, I said, "This student may tend to be a little perfectionistic." He said, "Isn't it all right to want to be perfect?" Caught me! We all want to be perfect. It's that drive of constantly making it better that makes us human and helps us to be mature.

The tendency to be perfectionistic is a quality, a character trait. Maybe it arises from insecurity, but it's something that is pretty well established by age four. What we need to work with here is a character trait that can be expressed in the more positive way. In the same way, laziness becomes patience. Anger becomes passion for justice. Asceticism becomes I don't know what, but it certainly provides a wonderful example to the rest of us when it is matured as a character trait.

Q. More time and energy for giving.

R. Exactly. The simple life. Henry David Thoreau surely is a good example. There's a long process. You can be sure that your housemate, your partner, is working with this. Probably your partner knows clearly that other people think, "I am too perfectionistic." Whereas there may be some resistance to this, at the same time there surely is some acknowledgment that "I could be more flexible than I am." So that consciousness is wearing away the rough edges to reveal the real jewel that is there, that particular individualistic jewel. It may take more than one lifetime.

Q. That's very helpful. Not to see the perfectionism as an obstacle in itself.

R. That's the present manifestation of a character trait that can be very wonderful and save everybody.

Q. Rōshi, you said that sometimes Dāna can be an act of selflessness, and sometimes it can be an act of selfishness. I remember walking from the beach, talking with a friend. At one point this person held out her arms and said, "I just love to give." [The speaker moved both arms, gesturing toward herself.]

R. Oh, really? With that gesture? [Laughter]

Q. Of course it was very funny. The words spoke one thing and the body said just the opposite. Can you suggest how we might catch ourselves short of doing this?

R. I don't think there's really a dividing line. An artist, a musician, or a dancer lives a life of giving, but each receives enormously. The Buddha himself received enormously. In the dokusan room I am constantly receiving in a way that renews my energy for giving.

I recently saw a TV interview of Placido Domingo, the Spanish tenor. He was so clear about his singing and what he receives from an audience. The more he gave of himself, the more enriched he was. The person who says, "I just love to give," is saying the same kind of thing, but perhaps at a more undeveloped level.

It's interesting in this regard to look at Kuan-yin because she embodies, as an archetype, this same two-way giving, except that, in her case, the more she receives the more she gives. Kuan-yin's name—Kannon, or Kanzeon in Japanese—means the one who perceives sounds. Or the one who perceives sounds of the world. She is realized—enlightened—by hearing, that is receiving those sounds. She is completely open to them. But because she is completely open, she is also open to the sounds of suffering in the world. So she is the archetype of mercy. Enlightened by all beings, she enlightens all beings. This is the archetype that we take to heart as the inspiration for our practice.

Q. Should we be concerned with the spirit of giving or with its result?

R. That's a baffling question. An artist just dances, sings, or paints. When you're with your friends, you just listen—you offer acknowledgment or, at times, correction. Is this spirit or result? When you try to analyze this, it's like Ikkyū tearing open the cherry tree to find the blossoms. They're not there.

Q. The term *codependence* has a Buddhist meaning and a modern psychological meaning. In the modern psychological meaning, it is "to give to receive," to create a pattern where your own self-worth is based on taking care of someone who will not take responsibility for him or herself. Can you comment on the Buddhist meaning and on the modern psychological meanings?

R. The term *codependency* in Buddhism is simply a word that points to how things are. Everything depends on everything else. *Codependency,* as a Western term, refers to a way of responding to drug abuse or alcoholism or some fixed neurosis in the family or among friends. To keep things moving smoothly, one goes along with or supports the other's fixation. No maturity is possible until somebody points out, "Hey, you're neglecting your children," or, "You're not allowing yourself to fulfill your own possibilities." Until someone can summon up the gumption to say such a thing or to indicate it some way, nothing happens. Inevitably, there is a kind of regression. Working with children, we know that sometimes we must put our foot down. But in dealing with peers, it's very hard.

Q. Does the act of giving always involve doling out? There are times when you actually hold back as an act of giving. Also, when you give anything, it has to be the right time and the right circumstance.

R. Yes, that's right. For example, I was talking with someone on the Big Island who had just written a novel. I asked, "Do you have a publisher? Do you have an agent?" She said she was *ho'ano* and explained that *ho'ano* is a Hawaiian word meaning "holding the seed."[13] She wasn't ready to talk about publishing. There are times when you must hold to yourself. As Dōgen Zenji says, you wait for the appropriate time because your gift cannot be completely effective if you just dump it out.

Q. The next question is, how do you know the right time?

R. Find the place of peace in your zazen, and your options become clear.

Q. In relation to what you were just talking about, could you say that if you are holding back from other people, you are giving to yourself?

R. In the example I gave of the woman who wrote a novel, I think it is more a matter of feeling that the gift can be truly effective at a certain time—and that time is not yet. She knows that once she has the contract in hand, she can talk about it. But there are also gifts to oneself. I give to myself when I go to the bookstore.

Q. You said something about giving and trust. Could you elaborate on that?

R. The spirit of trust is the spirit of Dāna. You trust others to turn the Wheel with you. You trust others to do well. You are giving them your power.

Q. In Theravāda Buddhism I've experienced Dāna in giving and receiving food, and it's a joyful experience. There doesn't seem to be as much joy in descriptions of Dāna in Mahāyāna practice. Where does joy fit in?

R. Well, I remember my own joy in sounding off with my teacher when he shouted "Kats'!" in the zendō. I did not consciously think, "This is joy," but I joyously joined his shout. It was his gift and mine. Afterward we were sitting there in zazen, and the Rōshi peeked around from his place behind me and said, "Oh, this one is enjoying his *Mu*!" Yes, I was sitting there filled with delight, although I could not have said, "This is delight."

Since we're on this subject, I want to say that religious practice, no matter what the religion, is not necessarily joyous. People on the path commonly have a hard time with fear, terror, misery, and pain. One goes through this.

Q. Is there any nourishment to the heart in this fear and pain? Or is it enough just keeping on with the practice?

R. The analogy is falling in love. When that initial experience is deep, there is something that sustains a couple and helps to carry them through whatever difficulties they may have. Now I'm not talking about satori or kenshō here, but there is an initial experience of finding oneself on the path that can be very profound.

In my own case, while I was in a Japanese internment camp

during the war, sick as a dog with asthma, I found R. H. Blyth's *Zen in English Literature.*[14] I must have read that book ten times, finishing it and starting again. I would have experiences at various places in the book—again, these were not kenshō experiences. I don't know what they were. I would be reading along and thinking, "Now I'm coming to the place where I had an experience before." I would come to the place, and it would happen again. Everything was transformed for me by those experiences, and to this day I am motivated by that book. All my writing springs from its style and intention. All my work comes from the profound vow that was made for me on reading it: that I would devote my life to Zen Buddhism, no matter what the difficulty.

TWO

MORALITY

The Shīla Pāramitā

The Second Pāramitā is Shīla, a term that literally means "cool and peaceful." It is the code of Vinaya, the moral way, and can be related metaphysically to the Three Bodies of the Buddha: the Dharmakāya, the Sambhogakāya, and the Nirmānakāya—the vast empty nature, the harmonious interdependent nature, and the infinitely varied nature of all beings.

The Dharmakāya is boundless vacancy, which is, at the same time, not a vacuum. Phenomena appear and quickly disappear. Nothing remains. With a perception of this reality, or with an understanding that such a perception is possible, I sense beginningless, endless peace.

The Sambhogakāya is interdependence with people, animals, plants, mountains, meadows, water, air, the planet Earth, the other planets, the sun, moon, and stars. My very genes are programs provided to me by my ancestors and from unknown sources back to the earliest green slime and before. Nothing is my own and everything makes me up: my parents, grandparents, birdsong, the portraits of Rembrandt, the scent of the Puakenikeni, and the clasp of my friend's hand. Also forming my being are death in the family, the danger of biological holocaust, and the misunderstandings that are inevitable in daily socializing. I am only my setting—interacting with all my past settings—nothing more.

The Nirmānakāya is my uniqueness and yours—and the unique formation of each leaf on a single tree. I have almost the same configuration as you but we have minute variations in our genes, experience, and memory to give us mysteriously distinctive individuality. With a perception of this reality, I sense my particular potential and yours—and the precious nature of each being.

The Buddha under the Bodhi tree uncovered the truths of ephemerality, harmony, and uniqueness. It was also clear to him that the anguish of the world arises from the human tendency to deny these fundamental realities and to cling instead to false notions of permanence and domination. So he devised the Eightfold Path and the Codes of Vinaya to guide his followers toward seeing into the same verities he had come to understand.

The Classical Code of Vinaya was developed from earlier Indian and Persian Precepts and consisted of five injunctions: not to kill, not to steal, not to misuse sex, not to speak falsely, and not to give or take drink or drugs. Known as the Pañchashīla, these five basic Precepts are accepted by monks, nuns, laymen, and laywomen in all schools of Buddhism. With the development of the Mahāyāna, five additional Precepts were added: not to speak of faults of others, not to praise the self while abusing others, not to spare the Dharma assets, not to indulge in anger, and not to defame the Three Treasures.[1] The total roster in the Mahāyāna is called the Bodhisattva Precepts, or the Ten Grave Precepts.

Zen Buddhist ritual and monastic practice traditionally acknowledges the importance of the Precepts. The literature does not include much about them specifically, but over and over we find sharp reminders that we are living in this world with other beings:

A monk asked T'ou-tzu, "All sounds are the sounds of Buddha—right or wrong?"

T'ou-tzu said, "Right."

The monk said, "Your Reverence, doesn't your asshole make farting sounds?" T'ou-tzu then hit him.

Again the monk said, "Coarse words or subtle talk, all returns to the primary meaning—right or wrong?"

T'ou-tzu said, "Right."

The monk said, "Then can I call Your Reverence a donkey?" T'ou-tzu then hit him.[2]

In the dimension of primary meaning all sounds are the sounds of the Buddha and all talk illuminates his teaching. This is the vast and fathomless Dharmakāya. It inspires us at each moment but nobody lives there, just as nobody lives exclusively in the worlds of harmony or individuality. The monk delivered a couple of cheap doctrinal shots and got his comeuppance.

If the literature does not deal with the Precepts as such, Zen Buddhist ritual presents them unequivocally. The ceremony of accepting the Precepts, known as *Jukai,* begins with the Three Vows of Refuge in the Buddha, Dharma, and Sangha—realization, the path to realization, and the harmony of all beings. "I take refuge in the Buddha; I take refuge in the Dharma; I take refuge in the Sangha." These are the vows of all Buddhists everywhere and the Refuge Ceremony is the initiation into the religion.[3]

The student is then offered the Three Pure Precepts: to maintain the moral code, to practice all good Dharmas, and to save the many beings. In the first of these Three Pure Precepts, my vow is to follow the way of not killing, not stealing, and so on. Here I find the hard light of clear definition, the sharp navigational beam of noble speech and conduct. In the second of the Pure Precepts, to practice all good Dharmas, my vow is to express my love. Placing these two Pure Precepts one after the other, I am reminded that the negative and the positive express the same vow. Ahimsā is Karunā; Karunā is Ahimsā. Nonharming is love; love is nonharming.

Finally, the Third Pure Precept, to save the many beings, sets forth the function of the first two. It gives specific direction to my way of nonharming and love. Thus I turn the Wheel of the Dharma with all people, animals, and plants.

The Ten Grave Precepts then arise from the Three Pure Precepts and clarify the Buddha Dharma like this:

1. I take up the way of not killing. This first Precept balances the first of our "Great Vows for All": "The many beings are numberless; I vow to save them." The Precept is specific and negative in wording; the vow is universal and positive. I vow not to harm other beings. With this vow, and with the personal peace that comes with conscientious zazen, the difficult questions we face in our lives—from how to deal with vermin to how to deal with unwanted pregnancy—become clearer.

Thus the teaching and formal practice integrate with daily exigencies. We find that an absolute position—say, of never harming the roaches in the kitchen—will probably lead to harm in our families. But, on the other hand, ruthlessly and endlessly exterminating roaches to protect the health of our children can lead to a wishy-washy kind of relativism. The solution is, of course, for the family to keep the kitchen as clean as a Zen temple, so that the roaches must do their scavenging elsewhere. Then the occasional roach can be escorted outside.

Questions about unwanted pregnancy are not as easy. Again, one would hope that a quiet mind and the Buddha's teaching of nonharming can help the woman work through her crisis. Abortion is killing, but what are the implications of nonharming as an absolute commandment in each specific case? How about the mother who might be so burdened by an extra child that each of her other children is harmed . . . ? Indeed, that society generally is harmed, that the very Earth is harmed? The woman is feeling her place in the endless stream of procreation, finding her body responding positively to its role, dreaming of her infant at her breast. Men and even other women do not share her particular dilemma. It is our duty to stand by her in her predicament, support her decision, and offer her our help, if she should request it. We should also organize for a universal way of compassion and care that will keep such terrible predicaments to the smallest possible number.

On a larger scale, we must act as responsible citizens of

the world and deal with issues of war and the destruction of the planet. Incredibly murderous engines are ready to destroy all human life and almost all animal and plant life. So-called conventional weapons destroy entire societies year by year.

No less dangerous is the biological disaster suffered by forests, meadows, wetlands, lakes, rivers, seas, and the air, threatening the life of literally everything. How should one resist ruinous technology while supporting a family? This is the kōan one carries day and night. I vow to cultivate my love and to apply it in my daily life, at home and in the larger community. I vow to moderate my lifestyle for the protection of all beings. I vow to speak out decisively with like-minded friends.

2. I take up the way of not stealing. The integrity of others is violated by stealing. There is, moreover, a certain order of things, a certain harmony. The Sambhogakāya, the Buddha's "Body of Bliss," is the interbeing of mountains, rivers, animals, towers, people—and it functions in people by morality. We attend this moral order by following the Precepts. The books of my friends, for example, are their bodies, as much as their fingers and toes. I cannot steal a library book without violating lives. Like questions of abortion, the easy resolutions are elusive. I vow to find within myself the ground of respect for the integrity of each being and of each collective of beings. But of course respect for, say, skinheads or neo-Nazis does not imply respect for their words and deeds.

3. I take up the way of not misusing sex. It seems that Classical Buddhism limited this Precept to a careful exposition of where, when, and with whom sexual intercourse is appropriate. But, beyond such rules, the misuse of sexual intercourse is the lie of giving, when the act is really taking. With such a lie, the entire relationship is a lie. And there are other ways to misuse sex than just in the sexual act. A relationship that involves dominance, exploitation, and passive aggression is an ongoing violation of this Precept. The drive to tear the other down can be so overtly violent that the malefactor lands in criminal court, but each of us can find this Māra, this Destroyer, lurking in our motives and responses. Get thee behind me, Satan! Honest sex, the easy joyous act and relationship, is Dāna, the gift that brings happiness to the world and to the family.

4. I take up the way of not speaking falsely. Like every other Precept, not speaking falsely is simply a particular aspect of not killing. Here the vow is not to kill the Dharma, the truth of how things are. I lie to defend my false notion of a fixed entity—a self-image, a concept, or an institution. The situation becomes confused and the reality that the Buddha revealed becomes obscured. Sometimes, however, I feel that I must lie to protect someone else or large numbers of others. Am I lying to myself? It is all too easy. I vow to find the big picture and then to be true to that discovery.

5. I take up the way of not giving or taking drink or drugs. This was originally an injunction against wine. My teacher, Yamada Kōun Rōshi, would refuse a social drink of saké. If his host insisted, he would accept a tiny amount, touch it to his lips and put it down again. At his level of Japanese society, such conduct bordered on rudeness, but he was not one to neglect his vows.

By extension today, of course, the Precept also refers to drugs. I have heard friends take a righteous position about cocaine: "It makes my mind more alert and helps me to communicate better." Maybe so in occasional instances and in the very short run, but cocaine is empirically provable to cause confusion over time and to be harmful to personal and social health. The same is true of alcohol. By indulging, you encourage others to indulge. Don't take drugs and don't give them to others. Don't cloud your mind or encourage others to cloud theirs.

6. I take up the way of not discussing the faults of others. More people get hurt by gossip than by guns. The point is that nobody has a fixed character. Everyone has traits, tools of character to be used or misused. If I have a tendency to be accommodating to other people, I can misuse this trait in a self-centered way as a means for personal protection. On the other hand, I can accommodate people in a manner that is clearly beneficial to them. Character transformation is not a matter of changing traits. It is rather taking my innate configurations and making the most of them. I vow to understand and encourage the fundamental qualities of my character and of others.

7. I take up the way of not praising myself while abusing others. The reason I praise myself and abuse others is that I seek to justify and defend myself as a superior being. Actually, I am not superior or inferior. The Buddha himself is not superior, and Māra, the Destroyer, is not inferior. "Comparisons are odious." If I am authoritarian and put myself up and others down, then I am not meeting their need to grow and mature. I am not meeting my own need to listen and learn. The world is multicentered and we're all in it together. I vow to follow the way of modesty and to take joy in the liberation and attainments of others.

8. I take up the way of not sparing the Dharma assets. The Dharma assets are phenomena in their precious uniqueness, the perfect harmony of their interdependence and their absence of any abiding self. When I am not stingy, then I conduct myself and say things that enhance my function as an avatar of the Buddha and I enhance that same function in others. My family members, friends, and everyone and everything are heartened on their path of perfection. My act of sparing the Dharma assets, of withholding money, goods, help, and ordinary decency, leads to pain and grief across the world. I vow to be generous.

9. I take up the way of not indulging in anger. Those of us who have attended religious retreats have had the experience of bathing in anger. Something unreasonably tiny, perhaps something we don't even notice, punctures a nasty bubble of angry gas and we sit there on our meditation pads playing out scenarios of retribution. However, this condition fades and the experience reveals the power of anger and its possibilities. Blake said, "The tygers of wrath are wiser than the horses of instruction." Kuan-yin hurls a thunderbolt of anger from time to time. I vow to find the place of equanimity where my anger can come forth to save everybody and everything.

10. I take up the way of not slandering the Three Treasures. Slander of the Three Treasures is Wrong Views: denial that there can be such a thing as liberation from anguish, denial that practice is a virtue, and denial of friendship. This is the ultimate destruction of the Buddha Dharma and of happiness in the world. Conceptualizing the Three Treasures and making them into a kind of structure that can be admired only from outside is another way of slandering them. I vow to practice Right Views as I stand up, sit down, and greet my family members and friends.

The Vinaya is the first basket of the Tripitaka. It is Ahimsā, nonharming, set forth by Shīla and its Precepts. It is morality beyond formal regulation. Without it, the Buddha Dharma does not apply and is not relevant. Sutras and commentaries are isolated and cold. With the light of Ahimsā, however, Karunā—compassion—finds a way.

QUESTIONS AND RESPONSES

Q. Can we realize our original nature without these Precepts? Can a person awaken without practicing?

R. Of course. It's like asking if you can have sex without love. You can have an experience, but it needs a frame; it needs a human body, so to speak.

Q. In the moment of realization is one practicing the Precepts?

R. The moment of realization is just the birdsong, just the call of the gecko.

Q. Then it has nothing to do with the Precepts?

R. Nothing to do with anything. Only that birdsong, only that call of the gecko.

Q. Then the Precepts are something man made to guide himself to his realization?

R. Realization is also the result of human guidance. The experience of realization comes with aspiration applied in zazen, hearing teishōs, and so on. Of course, Precepts are part of that context. The point is that the experience itself is grace, and by itself it has nothing to do with anything else. Still, you set yourself up for grace with your practice and afterward you carry on with the help of the Precepts, teishōs, zazen, dokusan, and the advice of your friends and family.

Q. To what extent is moral action spontaneous—not labored or considered, but spontaneous? In a Christian or a Buddhist context, if a person is suffused with grace, would their actions inevitably be moral?

R. Christian or Buddhist Precepts provide structure and guidelines to the perennial, that is, to what we already know in our heart of hearts to be noble and beautiful. A friend of mine said to another friend, "Robert Aitken is really a closet Confucian." When that got back to me, I was quite taken with it. Quite apart from the way Confucian teachings have been used to maintain male dominance in Asian families and political control in Asian governments, the Confucian ideal is human nobility. One could do worse than be a closet Confucian, I thought—a lot worse. And to answer more specifically, I think grace inspires the Precepts and the Precepts inform grace. This is a process, a practice, and as it becomes internalized, it will tend more and more to be spontaneous.

Q. We practice to develop an awareness, so that we can act in an honorable way, using the Precepts. But we will always be working at some level of imperfection. What is acting honorably in daily life?

R. This matter of honor is very interesting. In Zen Buddhist literature, we find the teacher addressing a beginning student as "Honored Sir," the way Senzaki Sensei used to address us as "Bodhisattvas." Honor is directly related to nobility, not the social class of nobles, but as the Buddha used *noble* in setting forth the Four Noble Truths and the Eightfold Noble Path. It is the highest and best to which we can aspire. Indeed we aspire and conduct ourselves as imperfect beings. We share the nature of the Buddha Shākyamuni. If he had been perfect, he never would have had to seat himself under the Bodhi tree. He would never have had to struggle with visions of demons and dancing maidens in his zazen. All beings by nature are Buddha, we are told. But the Buddha was and is human.

Q. Part of morality is that one should fulfill his or her function in life in a noble way. Take Rembrandt. He was an artist, creating great art that is appreciated even to this day. And his family life was quite good. He was a moral person, and so was Bach. We see a lot of people in history who fulfilled their function in life and were honest in doing it. How can people be moral in our present society when so many people are rewarded for stealing?

R. I appreciate your example of Rembrandt, who was perhaps the greatest Western artist of all time, or one of the two or three greatest—and also a noble human being. One can't help making invidious comparisons with certain modern artists whose personal lives have been a mess. I agree that it is tough to be moral in today's world, where people do indeed seem to be rewarded for stealing. It comes down to practice. There are two kinds of people: those who practice and those who don't. And what is your reward? The proverb says, "Virtue is its own reward," which is more enjoyable than it sounds.

Q. Individuals and corporations often buy large areas of land and clear it for construction, leaving less and less of the natural habitat for other beings. Do you see that as a violation of the First Precept of not killing?

R. Yes, but fundamentally it is not the Precept that is violated but the beings who are killed and the habitat itself that is damaged or destroyed. And where do you draw the line? Some trees have to be cut. Even beavers know that. When I did one of the early rounds of teishōs on the Precepts, one of my students came to me afterward and said, "Even cutting a flower is stealing." So I worked that into my later teishōs. But that student is a professional flower grower. What do we do with the filter after we have removed all the microscopic wiggly things from our water? Absolute adherence to any one of the Precepts is death. You can't treat them in a completely strict way. At the same time, you can't be wishy-washy. So the Precepts are kōans for us.

Q. I'm finding myself reacting to your statement that abortion is killing.

R. Now we're getting down to cases. Of course it's killing, but. . . . It's very difficult to make any generalization about abortion. I take joy in recent news that certain groups have been encouraging communication between the two sides of the controversy. It seems to me that often the woman finds herself left out. On the one hand, there is a tendency to deny that there is really a problem for the woman, no sense of tragedy and responsibility for cutting off the stream of life that has come down through the woman from primordial times. On the other hand, there is the denial of profound human tragedy that too often is involved in letting this child be born. I am really happy that there is at last some move to bring the two sides together. A lot of letting go is necessary here, it seems to me.

Q. How does the precept of nonstealing apply to Robin Hood?

R. Subtleties within subtleties. Self-deception within self-deception too. In Robin Hood's time and place, in the time and place of mythology, Robin Hood was and is a symbol of resistance to the organized system of greed that keeps classes apart and creates suffering among the poor. We can learn from his story the importance of such resistance—though our particular style of resistance, informed by meditation, Precepts, and experience, is likely not to involve robbing and killing.

Q. Could you elaborate on the precept of sexual misconduct, especially on some issues regarding committed couples? How do we deal with our various sexual feelings? Can sexual misconduct occur in a committed relationship?

R. No, because the spouse abuser is not committed. Let me say more about commitment. There are innumerable kinds of people in the world, and so there are innumerable kinds of relationships. I am acquainted with someone who was in a three-cornered relationship, two men and a woman. It finally came to an end, but it was viable for about twelve years. They were happy and there were no more tensions than in a normal family—a statistically normal family. So who's to judge?

I was talking about all this with my son one day. He said that he thought there can be a committed one-time sexual encounter. I think he's right. The Precept is not a commandment; it's a light on the path. What I mean by committed may not be what you mean. The real test is: How does a relationship contribute to my practice and the practice of the others, including all others, not just my partner? Does it contribute to our task of making real the innate harmony of all beings? And you don't have to make judgments from scratch. You can even learn from statistics. Just studying the numbers, I am sure you would find, say, that open marriage doesn't work. But statistics about sexual relations do not necessarily justify legislation.

Q. I feel that we know what sexual misconduct is in ourselves; there's a kind of inner knowledge that guides us, though I don't know where it comes from. But also, I think it's important for us to speak openly to the issue because many people, especially gay and bisexual people, are very confused and hurt by society's sense of morality.

R. Exactly. Conscience becomes confused with public opinion. *Conscience* means "the sense we have in common." This sense is informed—*given form*—by culture, which means that it can be informed by homophobic prejudice, as you say. The inner knowledge of which you speak is the place of peace and harmony you find in your heart with your practice of zazen and with your intimate experiences of love in your family and your Sangha.

Q. When someone is speaking ill of another, we want to refrain from joining in, but what if one needs to speak up?

R. I try to remember to suggest that the speaker take up the matter with the person being discussed. I don't always succeed in remembering this, though it is certainly something I would want if I myself were the topic.

Q. Regarding the Precept of not praising yourself when abusing others—you mentioned authority and authoritarian relationships. In the Zen Buddhist relationship of teacher and student, and in the relationship of father and child, sometimes there is a sincere desire for good, out of love for the other. But when it is authoritarian love, the other is confined. How can we deal with this?

R. Of course that is the danger of parenting and of Zen teaching as well—of infantilizing the other. One good way out is to build in some kind of role-reversal procedure, like our Dharma encounter ceremony, when you come forward one by one and make presentations. The real Dharma encounter would be one of you sitting here and me coming up to ask a question, but our way is pretty close to that ideal. Some people delight in challenging me in the dokusan room, and that's fun for me too.

You can change roles in the family. I have told about a Quaker family I lived with for a while. The mother and daughter would argue fiercely, but suddenly one of them would switch and take the other side. Then the mother would be whiny and the daughter would be bossy. They would break up and laugh and talk it over. It worked in this family; perhaps it could work in your own.

Q. What do you do when authoritarianism comes up with a Sangha friend?

R. I think that your transference is probably less intense, so you could bring the matter into the open more easily than you could with a teacher or a parent.

Q. What if they don't buy it?

R. You've done your best. It might sink in later.

Q. Would you go over the Eighth Precept again?

R. Yes: Not Sparing the Dharma Assets. There are many ways to understand it. In *The Mind of Clover* I mentioned one of the more classical ways of understanding it. That is, you don't spare money and other things in support of the Dharma. But really, there are many Dharma assets, Dharma virtues, that are important for you to embody and express. Don't hold back, in other words. Without being narrow or sectarian, your manner and your words should be expressive of the Buddha's wisdom. You convey the Dharma in your manner, in your punctuality, in your dress, in your devotion to your work, in your attention to others, and so on. This is conveying the Dharma, and that is what the Precept is about.

Q. What does it mean to indulge in anger?

R. It's when you brood about some injustice and don't even try to come back to your practice in meditation, or to your work or social interaction. Whatever you do is colored by this brooding.

Q. In other words, when anger becomes a distraction in your daily life, it's an indulgence?

R. When you pump it up, it's an indulgence.

Q. I doubt if anger ever deflates entirely, but can we learn to redirect it?

R. Sure. I always think of Yasutani Rōshi in this connection. He was taken to a Buddhist temple for adoption by the priest when he was five years old because his family couldn't afford to keep him. This must have instilled deep anger in his heart. He was always in trouble, fighting with his fellow little-boy monks. Although he did very well in his Buddhist practice and actually became a lecturer on Buddhism in the Sōtō school, he felt very resentful because none of the promise that had been held out to him had been fulfilled in his life. Then after he was forty years old, he finally found Harada Rōshi who helped him through his first realization. He gradually settled down into the practice and by the time he was sixty-five he was an independent master. But when you see pictures of him while teaching, you can see passion in his manner. His anger was transformed into passion in teaching. He never lost any of that early feeling, but it was transmuted. Be grateful that you have anger. Be grateful that you have sexual drive, and so on. These are your passions, your energy. How will you use them?

Q. It seems to me that there is a dharmic place for anger that is not self-centered.

R. We discuss this about once every two months at this zendō. My example is the parent who says to a child on the kitchen table, "Get off of there!" and the child gets off and doesn't try it again. It's very instructive, that tiger of wrath.

Q. Do you feel that guided anger is an indulgent kind of thing?

R. When the resource person or leader is skilled, it can be therapeutic. At the Maui Zendō some years back we had a whole summer of Gestalt. Some people were put off by our enthusiasm, but we actually got a lot of good work done. You touch those smelly bubbles of angry gas and pop them.

Q. But doesn't that create more of them?

R. A skilled leader can guide you right through it.

Q. Do you think people can get cleaned out of their anger?

R. The transmuting process does not involve emptying yourself of emotion. It's a matter of recasting. It takes work, and is best done openly within the safe environment of an established ritual with others, such as those found in the human development movement and the reconciliation observances of Theravāda Buddhism. Once you understand how these rituals work, you can use them everywhere, formally and informally, in family and workplace.

Q. My grandfather was a preacher. He was supposed to be a good man, yet he had such moral wrath and indignation. I see a lot of anger in the various groups and activities in the peace movement. I feel that militarism is wrong, but sometimes in working with people I get confused because I allow myself to dump all my unexpressed feelings on a particular evil—whoever he, she, or it may be.

R. A. J. Muste is said to have remarked, "A pacifist is someone who goes to a peace meeting and gets into a fight." How to channel one's anger! You can't really repress it, you know. It just goes down in the basement and churns around there and becomes corrupt. Then it emerges unexpectedly and inappropriately. So I vow to find the place of equanimity where my natural anger can come forth in a seemly way. *The Diamond Sūtra* says, "Dwell nowhere and bring forth that mind," relevantly, with my human passion—in *this* circumstance, in *this* circumstance. Then I vow to notice how appropriate or inappropriate my action was, to come back to my practice of nowhere, to notice and check myself again, and return—and in this way to mold my anger into a true teaching tool.

Q. If we constantly stimulate the "don't do it" nerve cells of a child, that child will want to do the very things he or she is not supposed to do. Can the Precepts be defined in a positive way? Instead of saying "don't steal," say, "Respect your neighbor's possessions?"

R. It is clear to me that there is virtue in both the negative and the positive. The first two of the Three Pure Precepts are to avoid all evil and practice all good. I don't think you can have one without the other. The negative is the body, so to speak, without which you cannot act. The positive is the spirit, which gives you freedom, yet you are limited by your body. So in our Jukai ceremony in the Diamond Sangha, the postulants read the classical vow, which is negative, and then they add a phrase or sentence of their own, which interprets the vow. So the first vow might come out like, "I take up the way of not killing—to support people, animals, and plants, and to encourage their fulfillment."

Q. What is morality? When faced with a decision—what is right? what is wrong?—what action can I take that will bring unity and at the same time make each individual more him- or herself than the person was before?

R. It seems to me that we create unity and enrich others by making harmony more evident with our manner and words. This helps people to appreciate their own precious uniqueness and the precious uniqueness and variety of others. And what brings love and unity? It was Thoreau, of all unlikely people, who said, "The only remedy for love is more love." What brings love? Love!

And how does one negotiate from a moral position in the face of power that is not necessarily moral? This is implicit in your question, it seems to me. There is a natural tendency—at least I find it natural—to back off and avoid confrontation. Yet many other people and things may be dependent upon one person taking a stand in the face of a malignant power. The Quaker injunction "Speak truth to power" is one that I need to remind myself about frequently.

Q. The Buddhist idea that we're whole and complete as we are means that we already integrate and embody the Precepts. In a situation where we need to make a decision, should we trust that we already have the right answer inside of us and that we can allow that answer to come out?

R. That's an interesting point. What we have is a sense of what's right. The Precepts and our experiences help to guide that sense. Parents and nursery school teachers know that there's no one with a keener sense of justice than a small child. "His piece is bigger than mine!" How many times have you heard that! The little child's faculty may be self-centered or immaturely applied, but the basic sense of fairness is there clearly. It's conditioning that helps to sharpen what is already there, and it is also conditioning that helps to cover it up.

Q. The Precepts really depend on zazen for their application; in other words, zazen, or *compassionate action,* is what gives us the power to apply the Precepts meaningfully. It's the difference between making them live and having them be a set of rules that have no life.

R. Yes, I think your point about Precepts depending on zazen is important. How do you find that they depend on zazen?

Q. Well, for example, you can look at a tree with compassion and attention, or you can look at it in a way that's cut off and superficial. Which way you look at things in general will determine whether the Precepts are something you can apply or whether they're just rules that have no power.

R. Yes. That is a point other than what I thought you might be making, but it's also very important. When we give the other our full and undivided attention, we can't help being empathic.

It's when we look away or close our ears that we can't respond in a way that reflects our unity.

I remember the difficulty I went through once when I was walking in San Francisco and came upon a ragged man on the sidewalk. He was ashen in color and obviously very ill. He said, "Could you call me an ambulance?" I remember how revolted I was by his appearance and by his smell. I had really to take myself in hand, go into a store, and get the proprietor to call an ambulance for him. How is it that I was not able to give him my full attention? I hope that I could do better now. I think maybe I could.

But you know, another point about zazen and the Precepts is that with zazen you not only cultivate attention but also reach a place of true quiet. Things are not buzzing; things are not hectic at all. Even with war and rumors of war, there is something in your heart of hearts that does not move and is always at rest. In that place of peace, you can say clearly, "I will do this; I will not do that."

THREE

FORBEARANCE

The Kshānti Pāramitā

Kshānti, translated as "forbearance and endurance," is the Third Pāramitā. This is not merely control of impatience, but the virtue that appears in the absence of hatred, repugnance, and malice. Like the other Pāramitās, it is an attitude that arises from Bodhichitta rather than from guidelines imposed from outside.

Kshānti has three aspects: gentle forbearance, endurance of hardship, and acceptance of truth. Gentle forbearance is the spirit of forgiveness. Injury is forgiven and the occasion is used as an opportunity to reveal the essential harmony of all beings. There are no exceptional circumstances that would justify other kinds of responses. The Bodhisattva remembers the Buddha's words, "The strength of a religious teacher is in his patience."[1] This strength plays itself out in teaching the Dharma, not in self-aggrandizement or protection.

The Head Monk Tzu-hao asked Fa-yen: "In opening this hall as a teacher, from whom do you have succession?"

Fa-yen said, "Ti-ts'ang."

Tzu-hao said, "You have turned your back on our late teacher Ch'ang-ch'ing."

Fa-yen said, "I still don't understand one saying of Ch'ang-ch'ing."

Tzu-hao said, "Why don't you ask me about it?"

Fa-yen said, " 'In myriad forms, a single body is re-

vealed.' What is the meaning of that?" Tzu-hao lifted up his whisk.

Fa-yen said, "That is what you learned from Ch'ang-ch'ing. What is the Head Monk's own opinion?" Tzu-hao said nothing.[2]

The dialogue continues, but this is enough for our purposes. Tzu-hao and Fa-yen had been brother monks, studying under Ch'ang-ch'ing. Fa-yen went on pilgrimage, where he encountered Ti-ts'ang and in their exchange, recorded in Case 20 of the *Book of Serenity*,[3] he suddenly saw an important point and remained with Ti-ts'ang and became his successor. Here Tzu-hao takes him to task rather strongly for betraying their late teacher by leaving him, but notice Fa-yen's response. He does not say, for example, "Hey, you know, it's all right to change teachers. There is plenty of precedent for such action. Besides, our old teacher gave his blessing to it." No, without even the mildest words of excuse, he grasps his chance to turn the Wheel of the Dharma and, by making a self-deprecating comment about something their late teacher said, leads Tzu-hao into a Dharma dialogue. His presentation of Kshānti continues to turn the Wheel for us today.

In Chinese the ideograph for Kshānti is formed with a sword over the heart. This emphasizes the Pāramitā as endurance of hardship. We live even in our most joyous moments with the sword of Damocles dangling above us by a single hair. The picture of our companion is on our altar as we hold our memorial service. Last year, last month, we had no idea that our friend would disappear into a photograph. You and I too will disappear into photographs soon enough. The full acceptance of this fact of life is Kshānti. It is the way of the Buddha and is taken on by the monk as a robe, the Kashāya, or Kesa. It is taken on by all of us as lay Buddhists.

Not only is life short; it is also hard. Here is the response of the poet Bashō to hardship. He has taken shelter during a storm in the rude dwelling of a frontier guard while he was on pilgrimage:

Fleas, lice,
The horse pissing
Near my pillow.[4]

Writing of this poem, R. H. Blyth comments, "Bashō's verse is to be read with the utmost composure of mind. . . . Sometimes, not by any means always, the simple elemental things, whether lice or butterflies, the pissing of horses or the flight of eagles, have a deep significance, not of something beyond themselves, but of their own essential nature. But we must lodge with these things for a night, for a day, for three days. We must be cold and hungry, flea-ridden and lonely, companions of sorrow and acquainted with grief. Bashō's verse is not an expression of complaint or disgust, though certainly he felt irritation and discomfort. It is not an expression of philosophic indifference nor an impossible love of lice and dirt and sleeplessness. What is it an expression of? It is the feeling 'These things too . . . ' But anyone who tries to finish this sentence does not know what Bashō meant."[5]

The poet Issa knew very well what Bashō meant. He wrote many poems about fleas and lice. Here is a familiar one:

I'm sorry it's so small
But please do practice your jumping,
Fleas of the house.[6]

On another occasion, Issa was leaving home to visit Matsushima, one of the most beautiful places in Japan:

Now you fleas!
You shall see Matsushima—
Off we go![7]

Issa's virtue, arising in the absence of repugnance, is plain good humor, where patience itself is forgotten.

This is the fulfillment of Kshānti and the fulfillment of the Buddha's basic teaching. "Duhkha, Duhkha," the Buddha said, "All is Duhkha," and he went on to teach the way of liberation from Duhkha. Usually Duhkha is translated as "suffering," but *suffering* is an ambiguous word that can mean *permission.* "Suffer the little children to come unto me," Jesus said. Let them come. Let it happen. Suffering is what Issa and Bashō experienced and they were not looking for liberation from it at all. The priest Issan Dorsey said, "To have AIDS is to be alive." The whole world is sick; the whole world suffers and its beings are constantly dying. Duhkha, on the other hand, is resistance to suffering. It is the anguish we feel when we don't want to suffer. The Buddha taught the Eightfold Path as the liberation from this anguish of futile self-protection. In this release we find the ultimate wisdom:

A monk asked Hsiang-lin, "What is the meaning of Bodhidharma's coming from the West?"
Hsiang-lin said, "I am stiff from sitting so long."[8]

This question about Bodhidharma appears again and again in Zen Buddhist dialogues. The reason he came from India to China, we can say historically, was to convey the Way of the Buddha. But the reason itself is not historical. "What is the Way of the Buddha?" the monk is asking. Hsiang-lin comes forth with the Kshānti Pāramitā. That very stiffness, that very tiredness is the reason. My teeth loosen and my hair turns white. My wife has arthritis in her hip and must use a cane sometimes. "What a comfort this cane is!" she exclaims.

Recently I spoke with a woman who had adopted a son from another country when he was still a baby. He had been kept in a crib for his first five months and today, at age thirteen, he has not attained reading and writing skills that would be average for his age. "But he lives with this as his nature and works with it," she remarked. This is the Noble Path of the Buddha.

The final aspect of Kshānti is acceptance of the truth. This is the way of working out Bodhichitta. It involves difficult, sometimes painful practice, a self-imposed limit upon the appetites and a drastic avoidance of ordinary worldly distractions. "Gradually you purify yourself," Wu-men wrote, "eliminating mistaken knowledge and attitudes you have held from the past."[9] Step by step you eliminate your ideas of a permanent soul, clarifying the oneness of life and death as you come to understand the unity of inside and outside. This is not just a philosophical practice and it is not just "working on yourself" in a psychological sense, though the intellect and the psyche have important roles.

The Buddha first tried philosophy, went on to asceticism, and finally took up the practice of exacting meditation. Though there was a certain sequence in this career, he did not reject the philosophical method or the asceticism he had practiced earlier. His philosophical training gave him tools, we can be sure, for the expression of the truth he uncovered under the Bodhi tree. He could not have held himself steady for his final work under the tree without his six years of disciplined asceticism.

In the *Cheng-tao-ke* (*Shōdōka,* "Song of Realizing the Way"), Yung-chia cites the Buddhist folk story of Shākyamuni living for many kalpas as an ascetic sage, Kshānti personified.[10] Ikkyū Zenji inscribed his poem on a painting of the Buddha as Kshānti:[11]

> *For six years hunger and cold pierced his bones to the marrow.*
>
> *Ascetic discipline is the mysterious teaching of the Buddhas and Patriarchs.*

I am convinced there is no natural Shākyamuni:
Now in the world, patch-cloth monks are just rice bags.[12]

This is Sonja Arntzen's translation. The term *genshi,* which Dr. Arntzen translates "mysterious teaching," can be rendered in a number of ways. *Gen* is also "initiated" and "expert." *Shi* is "instruction," but it is also "successful, splendid, promising." Ikkyū is giving a lofty place to ascetic practice. Without it, he is saying, even Shākyamuni would not have found his great realization. Without ascetic practice, Buddhist students were just rice receptacles in Ikkyū's day and perhaps he would have similarly scornful remarks about us in our time.

There is no natural Shākyamuni, no nature-made Shākyamuni, to use D. T. Suzuki's version of Ikkyū's words.[13] Practice is essential and it is ascetic, that is, it is willed self-discipline. The perfection of discipline is the peak experience of dropping off body and mind and there are many steps in preparation. This is not, of course, the asceticism of staring at the sun from a bed of nails, but it is rigorous nonetheless.

People sometimes ask me if they should get married or go back to school or take a certain kind of job. I answer in the affirmative when it seems to me that the plan is in line with their personal fulfillment. In our lay lives, career and marriage are part and parcel of practice. However, nobody ever asks me if I think they should go to a nightclub.

We are working together to establish lay Buddhism in the context of Western culture. I suppose it would be possible to continue the practice and the teaching at a nightclub, like Ikkyū himself, who visited such places. Or perhaps you can find a certain necessary relaxation and fellowship that is important for you. If the nightclub really is in keeping with the needs of your life as a student of Buddhism, by all means include it. It could even be a factor in prompting your realization, if you are ripened. One of my students had deep realization at a rock concert a week after returning home from sesshin.

Be careful not to deceive yourself, however. All beings by

nature are Buddha, which means your essential nature is peaceful and harmonious. Test your responses to your recreation. Is it truly re-creation? Time is passing and eventually you are going to have to get altogether serious. The human being is frail and vulnerable to accident and disease. Please don't wait for the oxygen mask!

I am thinking of a teacher from India who made many good points in his teachings and he made many mistakes too. Paramount among the latter was his neglect of asceticism. Therefore, fundamentally, there was no practice among his followers. Practice is ascetic—asceticism is practice.

All this may sound unreasonably demanding, but it is not. Leisure is part of practice. Our ideal is the royal ease of Kuan-yin and this is not something merely for the future. We do not work intensively without respite and then suddenly retire to royal ease. Leisure, sleep, vacation—these are practice too. In fact, according to Buddhist philosophy the highest and best Kshānti is the total release from hatred, repugnance, and malice that comes with realizing nothing itself. With this peak experience, you find rest and peace. This is the peace of Pu-tai (Hotei) entering the marketplace with bliss-bestowing hands.[14] It is your peace as you vaporize the gossip in your workplace or your practice center.

QUESTIONS AND RESPONSES

Q. What is the link between patience and harmony?

R. We are living the harmony of life and death. We are dying but we are alive. We are living but we are dying. Our life is that harmony of life and death, our whole existence. Patiently we harmonize life and death.

I remember going to see my friend Bob Olson, whose picture is on the altar in the dokusan room, when he was dying of cancer in Seattle. He looked very bad. His complexion was almost green. He had to carry around a little bag because he didn't have control over his bladder. I said, "How are you?" He said, "I'm waiting." Wonderful patience.

On another occasion I expressed surprise when I learned from Nakagawa Sōen Rōshi that a very old-timer, a middle-aged monk in his assembly, was still working on *Mu*. Sōen Rōshi said, "He's waiting." We are all waiting, really.

Q. In the Christian and Hindu traditions, asceticism often carries the connotation of denial of the senses, and there seems to be a similar sort of denial in Zen—wearing dark clothing, not listening to music, not stimulating sensual pleasures.

R. Well, you can't do zazen in a tin can factory. When he was in Japan as a young man, Gary Snyder used to join his friends and sit in the main concourse of Ueno Station, a supremely busy transfer point in northern Tokyo. When a train came in people would thunder down these cavernous concourses—and there would be this little group of crazy people sitting in a circle. The travelers would suddenly have to part around them. I don't think Gary and his friends did this very often and I wonder how good their zazen really was—but it was a good demonstration, like Pu-tai entering the marketplace. But you can't really do that as your central practice.

We keep distractions to a minimum but Zen Buddhism is not sensory deprivation. I don't tell people not to listen to music. Bassui Zenji asked, "Who is hearing that sound?"[15] There are many other questions and cases in the literature that bear upon sense experiences. Without sense experience there's no realization. Dōgen Zenji said, "The ten thousand things advance and confirm the self—and that is enlightenment."[16] You put the monastery in the mountains and then you're open to the sounds of the cicadas and the birds and the wind and the rain.

Q. So it's just getting rid of distraction?

R. Excessive distractions, yes. There is nothing more distracting in zazen than the human voice. For this reason, we have a rule about not speaking during sesshin. On the other hand, natural sounds are messengers, or can be, if you are open to them.

Q. It seems like that train station is a metaphor for many of our lives, full of noise, full of distraction. Is realization only available to those of us who can be free of such distractions? It sounds like practice might end up as an elitist thing.

R. Well, that's another tension. Ikkyū Zenji said, "I am convinced there's no natural Shākyamuni." So there needs to be some retreat. This can be part of your daily life, just half an hour, or periodic all-day sitting or longer sesshin. One of the things I learned from Katsuki Sekida was one-breath zazen. Just a breath before you pick up the phone, a breath after you put it down. It's like a child's picture that's made by connecting the dots. Each dot is a point of retreat or recollection. Then suddenly there's the whole picture.

Q. Potentially a prisoner in a clattery cell block could string together all those moments.

R. Yes, exactly. There is a story in a recent issue of *Turning Wheel* about an inmate who did zazen in a closet. Even before that story appeared one of my students at the Waiawa Community Correctional Facility was getting up an hour early and sitting in a broom closet.

The life of Brother Lawrence is very instructive. He was a seventeenth-century Carmelite monk who grew up without much education at all. When he was eighteen years old he had a religious experience quite spontaneously on seeing a tree in bloom. But circumstances were not right for him to do anything with his experience. He was drafted into the army and was wounded in battle. After he was mustered out, he worked many years as a groom. Remembering that youthful experience in middle life, he felt he must do something about it. He became a monk and was assigned to the monastery kitchen. He determined on his own that he would learn to find the presence of God in his busy kitchen as well as he could in the sanctuary. For ten years he endeavored to fulfill his vow without any success. Finally, he just decided: "I don't care if it takes another ten years or twenty years, or if it takes me the rest of my life, or if I never find the presence of God in busy circumstances, I'm going to keep trying." And with that, suddenly everything turned around, and he was indeed able to find that presence with him at all times.[17]

Q. I don't want this to come across too harshly, taking on two old boys with one bite, but I don't quite trust either you or the Buddha. Sometimes it seems to me that both of you do one thing and then say another. The Buddha went through all of these practices and then told us not to do asceticism. You talk about one-breath zazen, but when I look at your life there are a good many sesshins packed in, one right after the other. These Zen activities are much more serious than just being mindful when we pick up the telephone.

R. My suggestion about the telephone is only an example. When I take up this matter with students, I mention several possible intervals during the day and then suggest that they work out their own intervals. Basically, however, your practice is fueled by Bodhichitta. When that is in place, techniques will follow naturally and it won't matter whether you are a monk or a layperson, or whether or not you have lots of leisure to practice.

In this connection, I think of my friend Mr. Tetsuo Hiyama. When he was a university student in 1957, he did a sesshin with Yasutani Rōshi and screamed *Mu* at the top of his lungs for the first few days until he ran out of voice.[18] He didn't go to bed at all. He sat up in a little toolshed. Bankei Zenji went to extremes too. He sat on a bare rock for months and ruined his rear end—and developed TB during the process. He said later that such asceticism was not necessary, and I suspect that Mr. Hiyama is also smiling now about all his youthful screaming.

But at the time, it was necessary for those men to do what they did, and it was necessary for the Buddha to go through his ascetic period.

Flora Courtois found the path because she was so highly motivated that she went all the way through it on her own without any formal ascetic devices.[19] Most people, however, need to guide themselves with methods that help them to stay on the path. I like to translate the seventh step of the Eightfold Path as Right Recollection rather than Right Mindfulness—right remembering. It is important to remind yourself about remembering. With some people the devices will take, and with some people they won't. And I sense that there are many devices out there that are waiting to be discovered.

Q. My point was that sometimes you have to ferret this out for yourself.

R. Yes, zazen teaches zazen. You have to ferret it out for yourself. I'm just offering crude models—you must do the refining.

Q. Which is the greater danger, to take one's zazen too seriously or not to take it seriously enough?

R. I suppose it is more dangerous not to take it seriously enough. If the motive is there, then the effort is there and the function is there. The motive can always be tempered. But if the motive is not there, then the effort and the function are not there either—and what have you got to work with?

Q. You speak about asceticism in Zen practice, of always coming back to the practice even if you don't feel it. But asceticism is something that's often misused in Zen.

R. Yes indeed, lots of things are misused in Zen practice, and that's one of them. It's a difficult practice. Some people give up and other people persevere but become unnaturally tough. It's important to be sensitive to your body and find the creative Middle Way. Our Rōhatsu sesshin is as demanding as any practice that we have—going to bed at 9:00 P.M. and getting up at

4:00 A.M. for more than a week. But this is not extreme. At some centers in Japan the monks go to bed at 1:00 A.M. and get up at 2:00 A.M. There are unnatural strictures even about using the toilet. This is unreasonable discipline and it seems likely that only very arrogant types manage to get through it. But here we are not recruiting and training samurai.

Q. When we cut loose from family or a social situation in order to practice, there is sacrifice involved in that, a kind of asceticism. Is that necessary for Zen practice?

R. Of course, leaving home has been a requisite of practice for the monks and nuns for many generations, and in fact the idiom for becoming ordained in Asian languages is "leaving home." We find this cutting off of family ties not only in Buddhist practice. It's right there in the New Testament. When Jesus' family appeared, he said, "Who is my mother?" That was a kind of asceticism. But we also must find the way of leaving home without leaving home, to practice in the family context.

Q. There is a difference between leaving home because one doesn't like one's family and the way of leaving home in which you complete your relationships. Eventually you may have to go back and do it anyway.

R. I agree. We find the Buddha himself reconciled with his wife and son after he became a teacher. But let me say a bit more about the metaphor of leaving home. Traditionally, new monks or nuns walked naked to the town dump, pulled out scraps of cloth, bleached them, dyed them with natural dyes, and then sewed them together to make robes. The robe then became home. This is our allegory—within the family or apart. It is our model of commitment, once and for all, to the way of practice.

Q. The Buddha had to go through seven years of asceticism before he could say, "I don't want asceticism." Someone else may find it necessary to have a couple of years of hedonism before they can see it is not a path.

R. That's all right. The Buddha was a hedonist for the first twenty-eight years of his life. But it palled. I said a little earlier that we are all different. This is only half of the story. We are also somewhat alike, alike enough so that I can say: You should avoid this and that. How are we alike? By nature, we are Buddha. By nature, there is equanimity and harmony potential there that we can realize and fulfill. So what are the things that are conducive to that fulfillment? What are the things that are not conducive to it? A lot more effort and a lot more mindful devotion is necessary than many people think.

Q. Isn't it sometimes possible to go to a nightclub and lose yourself in those decibels, in that cocoon of sound? Isn't it also possible to forget the self in the act of becoming one with the music and dancing? Or would that be different than sitting zazen? And if it is, what is the difference?

R. I read accounts of aesthetic experiences, of athletic experiences, of sexual experiences, which describe a kind of falling away of the self. They are analogous to realization, to the Buddha's own experience. But just as there are qualities of realization that don't check out at all, so there are various levels of understanding that can be attained in these analogous experiences that you will need to check out with a teacher you trust.

Q. Can going to a disco be therapeutic fun? It feels good and you're happy while you're doing it. You feel fulfilled. That's part of being human.

R. Of course you need recreation. But maybe you are deceiving yourself and just giving way to indulgence. There's a lot of scope for self-deception in the human psyche.

Q. How can we examine that self-deception? What are the key points when I can say, "Yes, I'm really lying to myself." Or "No, I'm trying to be straight?"

R. The Buddha didn't deceive himself about his situation as a prince. He knew that he could not practice in the palace. Sometimes it is just as clear to students of Zen Buddhism that they have to make changes in order to maintain and deepen their zazen. But sometimes it will not be clear. I've had three or four experiences with people in questionable occupations. One was with a woman who was a masseuse in one of those dubious parlors. She was really interested in zazen and she asked me, "Do you think that I can continue as a masseuse in that place and still practice zazen?" I said, "Yes, you can. But six months from now, you will either be doing zazen and you will have quit your job, or you will be continuing as a masseuse in that place and you will no longer be coming here." And I said precisely the same thing to two or three other people, including a man who was a partner in a liquor store. There are certain occupations and certain human activities that are ultimately incompatible.

Q. A few weeks ago you remarked that Hakuin said shit in the toilet is the radiance.[20] So it is the same thing with the sunset or Anna Banana's [a disco near the Koko An Zendō].

R. Yes, of course that's true in the dimension of empty oneness, where everything is the same. But in the dimension of practice where does the human psyche have the best chance? The smell of shit is not that bad. But the decibel count at a rock concert is extraordinary. When my student had a realization experience at a rock concert, that cured me forever of trying to make any kind of absolute statement about these things. The exception proves the rule, however. This particular fellow is rather special in that he's a poet and a musician, so he was really listening there and something happened. We can say it's all one and that anything is possible. And it's true. But the configurations of practice are such that a teacher can generalize and say it's better not to eat lots of meat, not to make a habit of going to discos, and so on. It's better not to break the Precepts.

Q. As laypeople, we need to develop sides of ourselves. Discos are a fact of life. Everybody growing up needs to learn about certain things if we are going to live in this society.

R. One taste of a bad pie is enough.

Q. That's making the assumption that a disco is a bad pie.

R. I'm saying that it is fine to get acquainted with the extremes in our society but one look can be enough.

Q. I've noticed in myself a tendency to become righteous when I'm overly ascetic. My cure is to go down to Burger King and buy a Whopper.

R. Of course pride in asceticism is an indulgence. Smile at yourself. You don't cure one indulgence by taking up another one. You can temper your tendencies without swinging to another extreme.

Q. How is it that Ikkyū, the least ascetic of Zen masters, has written a poem in praise of asceticism?

R. Ikkyū is an extraordinary figure who cannot be summed up easily. For those of you who are not familiar with him, he was an illegitimate son of the emperor—illegitimate in the sense that his mother, a courtesan, was banished from the court. He grew up in the very topmost level of society, but he was still a marginal person because of the stigma of his birth. His mother died when he was little. He was raised by an uncle and decided very early that he wanted to be a monk. He trained very earnestly. But being a marginal person, he was very suspicious about others. It is interesting to trace the growth of a person who has that kind of marginal heritage. One tendency is to join the establishment and become more establishment than the establishment—like Napoleon who was born in Corsica and became fanatically French, or Hitler who was born in Austria and became fanatically German, or Stalin who was born in Georgia and became fanatically Russian. The bravery of colonial troops is legendary, including the 442nd Regiment of Nisei Americans in World War II. But the shadow side of this fanaticism or bravery on the part of marginal people is their feeling that they really don't belong and their anxiety to prove that they do. Ikkyū was of another sort. He accepted the fact that he didn't belong and thus he was able to keep a critical and objective view of the establishment.

Ikkyū Zenji avoided what Senzaki Sensei used to call "cathedral Zen." He did accept appointment to be an abbot but he served only briefly and walked out. As he grew older he came to feel more and more that there was something wrong with the restrictive forms not only of the church, so to speak, but of the doctrine itself. So he liked to hang out with the whores and the publicans and the butchers. There's a great painting of Ikkyū by Hakuin with a skull stuck on top of his long staff.[21] He would walk into the bars and whorehouses with this. He wasn't completely giving way to what was happening there, but he was not divorcing himself or being superior. When he was in his seventies, he had a passionate love affair with a blind minstrel who was much younger than he was. He wrote many beautiful love poems to her. He knew very well that hard practice was necessary, but how could he say this and still do these other things?

We haven't yet come to understand this man Ikkyū completely. He was so open with himself, so ready to confess his own deviations and lusty appetites. He faced himself squarely without much support from friends. He was pretty much on his own, trying to find his way out of the incredible restriction that he felt while still practicing the True Way.

Q. The idea of forbearance brings me to a tension I feel in socially engaged Buddhism, which tells me there is a role for acceptance and a role for taking action. Could you comment on that tension?

R. You put your finger on it. The forbearance and permission involved here is acceptance of the truth. What we are seeing in the world is not in keeping with primal truth. Let's bring some harmony here as best we can. I'm sure that this Pāramitā could be misinterpreted as an excuse for not doing anything. I don't think that was the Buddha's intention. He didn't stay under the Bodhi tree. After seven days he got up, looked for his disciples, and from then on, for almost forty years, he walked through India turning the Wheel of the

Dharma for and with the many beings. Although he accepted wholeheartedly the state of mind of the people that he met, he wasn't satisfied with them.

Q. You speak about simple living as an environmental practice. I wonder if you might talk about it as an ascetic practice that is in itself a way to care for the world?

R. The way of the sage is ideal, it seems to me. Simple accommodations, simple transportation, simple food that maintains the body as part of the larger organism. That is surely our ideal. I'll tell you a related story about Gary Snyder and his friends at San Juan Ridge, near Sacramento: When gold prices rose during the 1980s, the company that had owned rights to the tailings from placer mining for a hundred years applied to the county for permission to rework the tailings. Gary and his friends appealed to the county council to deny the company a permit. In their statement they said, "We want to keep our way of life for ourselves and our descendants for the next thousand years." The county council members were stunned, of course, for they had never thought of conservation in that way. But if we keep the larger picture of space and time in mind, we will surely be drawn to the simplest possible way of life. Are we using up the world by taking this food or taking this mode of transportation?

Q. What did the county council decide?

R. They turned down the company's request for the permit.

Q. Many of us have jobs and lives that bring us in contact with what seems impossible or endless suffering. How can we practice patience in the midst of these demands?

R. You've really touched me with that question. In my prison visitation, I am exposed to the anguish of people who are locked up for many years, which in many ways ruins their lives. But some of them have learned patience and are my teachers. They have found a practice in the most difficult of circumstances. I think of Bashō's haiku about the patience that is really fulfillment, a poem I often cite and never use up:

Journeying through the world
To and fro, to and fro,
Cultivating a small field.[22]

FOUR

ZEAL

The Vīrya Pāramitā

The Fourth Pāramitā, Vīrya, is literally "The Perfection of Zeal" or "The Perfection of Vitality." The Sanskrit word *vīrya* is related to our English word *virile.* However, the Chinese translation *ching-chin* takes the word out of any gender limitation and gives it spiritual depth and strength. The first ideograph, *ching,* has several implications: "essential, unmixed or refined, spiritual," and is used in everyday language to mean "polished rice." It is found in such terms as "single-minded," "the essential point," "vigorous and strong," and "nobility of mind." (Incidentally, with this etymology we gain a sense of the religious and cultural importance of white rice in the East Asian diet.)

The second ideograph, *chin,* means "advance" or "urge forward" and is found in such expressions as "to make an assault" or "to advance in culture." Together the two ideographs are "the advancement of single-minded spiritual vigor."

With *shōjin,* the Japanese rendering of *ching-chin,* we find further richness in the etymology. One meaning of this term refers to meals of herbs, ferns, berries and tiny wild potatoes that presumably form the diet of sages who live in the mountains. Nowadays, eating rare herbs, ferns, berries, and wild potatoes can become a fad for wealthy gourmets, but the original meaning is to live the Tao of the Buddha as if one were already a sage, dwelling in modest accommodations and eating what is available while pursuing the Way in the most single-minded manner possible.

How does this etymology play out in practice? Here is Vīrya

personified in the monk Chien-yüan, pursuing the way single-mindedly:

Tao-wu and Chien-yüan went to a house to pay condolences. Chien-yüan rapped on the coffin and asked, "Living or dead?"

Tao-wu said, "I won't say either living or dead."

Chien-yüan said, "Why won't you say?"

Tao-wu said, "I won't say."

On the way home, Chien-yüan said, "Your Reverence, please tell me right away. If you don't I shall hit you."

Tao-wu said, "You can hit me if you like, but I won't say." Chien-yüan hit him.

Much later, after Tao-wu had died, Chien-yüan went to Shih-shuang and told him this story. Shih-shuang said, "Alive, I won't say! Dead, I won't say!"

Chien-yüan said, "Why won't you say?"

Shih-shuang said, "I won't say! I won't say!" With these words, Chien-yüan realized something.

One day, Chien-yüan appeared in the Dharma Hall with a mattock and walked from East to West, from West to East.

Shih-shuang said, "What are you doing?"

Chien-yüan said, "I am searching for the sacred relics of our late master."

Shih-shuang said, "On the billows of the great ocean, whitecaps swell to the sky. What do you search for as our teacher's relics other than that?"

Chien-yüan said, "That was good for my practice."[1]

Chien-yüan is caught up in Vīrya, rudely demanding instruction from Tao-wu in solemn circumstances, pursuing his doubt thereafter, forgetting everything else. He is carried away to the extent that he even strikes his venerable teacher. After his teacher dies, he takes his kōan with him to Shih-shuang and finds some realization. He is not satisfied with his understanding, however, and again rather rudely demands further teaching from Shih-shuang. His comment on his second experience acknowledges it simply as an important milestone on his continuing pilgrimage.

There is another point here. Chien-yüan was obviously preoccupied with death, as most of us are in our heart of hearts. Living or dead? What happens after death? Worry about this can be the "valley of the shadow of death," the "dark night of the soul." Walking through this dark valley is fearful, even terrifying, especially since the rod and staff of God have been put away and there is only the practice to follow. Take one step, then the next and your own Vīrya guides you.

Students find two problems with Vīrya. The first is: What should I do if Vīrya is not well developed? The second is: How should I maintain Vīrya in the workaday world, with all its demands and distractions? These are intimately related questions.

Vīrya, like patience, like sincerity, like inquiry, like Samādhi, builds with practice. As Yasutani Rōshi would say, five percent is enough to start with. If you have enough vitality and stick-to-it-tiveness to sit through twenty-five minutes of zazen, then you have a quite a lot of spiritual zeal. If you have the gumption to ask the teacher a probing question even though you think it might be considered irrelevant or rude, then you are well along on your pilgrimage.

Without worrying about adequacy or relevance, Chien-yüan plunged ahead. He really behaved quite inappropriately, rapping on the coffin in a dead person's home, hitting his old teacher, bringing a mattock into the Dharma Hall. However, he was not merely being confrontational. He was trying to find his Way.

The human being by nature is inadequate, practices zazen inadequately, realizes true nature inadequately. This is the Vīrya Pāramitā. On and on we persevere, like a small child determined to learn how to walk while continually falling down, or like a very old person getting up in the middle of the night, lurching from wall to wall to reach the bathroom.

Then how can you can find a way through the distractions of conventional society? I would suggest you ask yourself, "What is my purpose?" Everything follows from your response to this question. Flora Courtois felt impelled to search for the basic, all-permeating reality. This search led her to a practice of attention so close to traditional Zen Buddhist training that it brought her to a realization that Yasutani Rōshi readily confirmed twenty-five years later. The distractions in her life and the misunderstanding of her condition by her college teachers and friends actually drove her forward.[2]

Who is in charge here? Daily life experiences can always be instructive. The first lesson is that *distraction* or *obstruction* are just negative terms for your context. Circumstances are like your arms and legs. They appear in your life to serve your practice. As you become more and more settled in your purpose, your circumstances begin to synchronize with your concerns. Chance words by friends, books, and poems, even the wind in the trees bring precious insights.

Perhaps your circumstances involve looking after small children. Your ability to attend formal meetings is restricted. How can such a situation synchronize with your practice? It is as though you plan a picnic and then it rains. Other ways of recreation open out. Other ways of practice can open out when full-time participation in sesshin is not possible—and they will involve Vīrya.

Traditionally, Vīrya has three aspects: character formation, religious training, and altruism.[3] Character formation can be guided by others if we listen to their criticism. Rituals relating to character such as the Jukai ceremony can be very helpful. In a further effort to encourage character formation we hold Harmonies Rituals in the Diamond Sangha. These are based on the Six Harmonies of the Buddha: sharing a common space, sharing the essentials of daily life, observing the Precepts, using only those words that contribute to harmony, sharing insights, and respecting the viewpoints of others.[4] In the course of this ritual we make individual pledges to correct bad habits. As I write this essay, we have held the first three rituals: sharing a common space, sharing the essentials of life, and observing the Precepts. My vow for the first was to get organized, for the second was not to hide myself, and for the third, to be decent. I carry these pledge cards in my calendar book and look at them once in a while as reminders. I'm going to clean up my desk. I'm going to make that difficult phone call. I'm going to conduct myself appropriately, according to the needs of others and the circumstances. These basic efforts are acknowledgments and practical applications of Bodhichitta, my desire and the desire of the community for deeper and clearer realization.

Notice that the Harmonies Rituals are not a Zen Buddhist tradition. Life in the Zen monastery itself is considered to be formative—"rocks in a tumbler" is the traditional metaphor. This is a metaphor and model that does not work for us as lay students in the West. Thus we must reach further back into our roots, back to earliest Buddhism, back to the Buddha himself, to find the truly perennial Way.

The second aspect of Vīrya, spiritual training, is a matter of taking one's practice in hand—of not depending solely on the teacher or the Sangha or even on the practice itself to do it. In a Diamond Sangha teachers' meeting, we hit on the term "the *Field of Dreams* syndrome," after the movie of that name. This is the notion that "If you build it, they will come." In the movie, a farmer who is preoccupied by the Chicago Black Sox scandal is persuaded by a mysterious voice to build a ball field to bring the team members back to life. He builds it and sure enough, they appear—but that is the movie. In the reality of Buddhist practice, you have to keep building. It is not enough to come regularly to meetings and to sit there waiting for whatever-it-is to appear. Thoughts come and go, images come and go, memories come and go, fantasies come and go, apartments get decorated in the finest detail—and the years pass. The practice is not just to enter the hall, bow, and sit down. What then?

Moreover, the practice is not just settled, exacting meditation and realization. It is study as well. My own teacher, Nakagawa Sōen Rōshi, once said, "If I had to take an examination in Buddhism, I would flunk." This is the great weakness of Zen Buddhism and he knew it. I was well along in my practice before I read my first book on general Buddhism and I was already teaching before I seriously began to look at the Four Noble Truths and the Eightfold Path. Some Zen teachers tell their students not to read, out of concern that they not speculate. I would much rather have speculation around me than ignorance. I feel passionate about this point. If you are a Buddhist, what does that mean? How do you understand karma? How do you understand rebirth? What is Duhkha? What is the Mādhyamika? Who were the main teachers of Classical Buddhism after Shākyamuni? What was their teaching? Who were the first teachers of the Mahāyāna, or the Vajrayāna? What was their teaching? The pursuit of such questions can enhance your formal practice and open many doors in your life. Don't neglect study.

The third aspect of Vīrya is called altruism, but when you read the commentaries you find that a broad range of qualities is subsumed under this single heading. Follow-through, illustrated in the story of Chien-yüan rapping the coffin, is one of these qualities. It begins with the breath. I want to give the most circumspect attention to my breathing and to completing each breath. In, out, in, out. Follow-through is a matter of completing each breath and each action, leaving nothing half-done, including the many aspects of formal practice. When my actions become blurred, then continuity becomes my way—rather than each thing, each being, each moment. Continuity leads from childhood to maturity to old age to death. The thrush with its message has no chance to come through.

Another quality under this heading of altruism would be optimism and still another would be application. Confidence in myself as the Buddha's avatar builds with practice. I develop an eagerness to undertake difficult tasks. This is noble aspiration, I hope, and should be distinguished from vanity and arrogance.

Some portion of my work as a teacher is always given over to offering encouragement. I remember times of great discouragement in my own early practice and am eternally grateful to my teachers who always took my complaints seriously and gave me the support I needed. Now in turn it is my task to repay their kindnesses by diverting their encouraging words to my students, rededicating their wisdom and compassion.

On his great realization, the Buddha exclaimed, "All beings are the Tathāgata. Only their delusions and preoccupations keep them from testifying to that fact."[5] Tathāgata is the one who "thus comes"—another name for Buddha. Rid yourself of delusions and preoccupations and you've got it. You have a hard time with this because your nature is the same as his. He had to practice hard too. Don't give up!

QUESTIONS AND RESPONSES

Q. What do you mean by the question, "What is my purpose?"

R. Some students aren't sure why they are practicing, so I ask the question to encourage them to confront their lack of clarity and ultimately to give their hidden purpose some definition.

Q. You mean their big, special purpose?

R. Yes. How does it all hang together? What is the purpose of your work, your family life, your zazen, your social welfare activities, your all-the-rest-of-it? When your purpose is clearer, then it becomes clearer what your practice should be. If your purpose changes, then your practice might change too.

Q. If there's no fixed agent of perception, then there's no fixed agent to push up zeal or to push up purpose. Is that true?

R. It's hard to push up purpose or zeal or anything else. It evolves as you go. Let me give you an example. I was talking this week with a visitor interested in zazen. He was talking about developing his *jōriki,* his Samādhi power. I didn't feel that I should challenge him too much. However, if a regular student brought up the matter, I would ask, "How do you develop your *jōriki*?" I think it develops of itself when you do zazen.

Incidentally, the visitor saw that I was being a little reserved, so he asked, "How do you understand the term *jōriki*?" I said, "Becoming one with *Mu.*" He was quite surprised to hear that. Maybe he thought *jōriki* is some kind of samurai power.

Of course it is power, in the sense of *toku.* Do you know that word *toku*? In Chinese, it is *te,* the *te* of the *Tao-te Ching.* Another word for *toku* is *virtue.* It is the strength of character that arises from zazen, realization, and service.

Q. So *toku* is really Vīrya?

R. Yes, it is, and so is Samādhi power, *jōriki,* when it is used by Kuan-yin. Vīrya, *toku,* and *jōriki* turn the Dharma Wheel if they are used and are not just ends in themselves for the self.

Q. Rōshi, I don't have much *jōriki.* I sit for a long time and then I come to interview. I find I don't have the zeal to push the air out to make my voice heard. I'm kind of in a daze.

R. You are in a natural condition. Don't give it a thought. Sometimes people sit down in front of me and I have to ask them to speak up. I'm getting a little deaf, you know. But that's not an important matter. Just raise your voice a little at such a time. Come to think of it, I have done dokusan with a certain rōshi who always whispers in dokusan.

Q. Can we go back to purpose? How can I encourage my purpose to become more clear?

R. You can use the method set forth by Eugene Gendlin in his book *Focusing.* He recommends that you find yourself a lawn chair or chaise lounge where you can be comfortable. You ask, "What's bothering me?" You lie there and some revelation pops up and you just look at it and then, remarkably, something from under that pops up. So you look at that new revelation. You don't try to analyze any of these insights. You go on, and ultimately you hit bottom and realize, "That's what is bothering me." It usually turns out to be something that is totally unrelated in any logical way with the first thing that appeared.[6]

You can establish your purpose in a similar way. Don't try to do it on your zazen cushions. As you know, when you try to work on yourself in zazen, the problem just goes around and around in your cortex and nothing is resolved. Zazen is not the time for working on yourself. The time for working on yourself is when you're semi-prone. Not prone, because you go to sleep. So lie back when you are alone and consider what your purpose might be. A fairly matter-of-fact purpose will appear and you just look at that. Then a deeper purpose comes up and you can finally get at your basic aspiration, at least for now.

Q. After uncovering these layers of purpose, what if you get to the question of "alive or dead?" What is the appropriate place to work on that question?

R. On your cushions in zazen. It was Chien-yüan's kōan. He rapped on the coffin and asked, "Alive or dead?" Tao-wu replied, "I won't say! I won't say!" That can be your kōan.

Q. You don't work on that semi-prone?

R. You can, but I wouldn't think you could get anywhere because, as you say, you have already reached the limit of semi-prone practice. But try it for yourself. Can you really do zazen in a chaise lounge?

Q. The point of zeal here, it seems to me, is not to practice that zeal outside of oneself.

R. Yes, but, you know, if old Chien-yüan had been inhibited by the thought, "Well, is this going to be outside myself or not?" he could never have rapped on the coffin. Right?

Q. But he could have asked himself, "Is this outside of myself or not?" And he could have asked that with a great deal of zeal.

R. Do you mean, "Is this coffin outside myself or not?"

Q. No, I mean, "Is this action outside myself?"

R. Then you are just turning back onto yourself. Chien-yüan really wanted to know about life and death! Lying there in the coffin—is the person alive in any way? That's what he's asking. The action of rapping is neither inside nor outside, or it is both inside and outside. Musing on the question of inside or outside at such a time is like musing about any aspect of your activity. This kind of musing is the function of your superego: to keep you straight. On your cushions, however, it leads to brooding. I hear a lot of superego in the dokusan room, that is to say, the voice of conscience—or the voice of caution, or the voice of doubt, the voice of criticism, mother's voice, father's voice. Maybe it comes out in a kind of existential framework, but it's really superego. Use it and don't be used by it.

Q. You talk about individual superego as being somebody else's voice pushing you, not your own.

R. It might be your own voice, it might be somebody else's. Actually, it is not anybody's voice but your own. You have made it your own, that is. You take responsibility for it. In any case, be glad that you have a superego. It is your sense of right and wrong. It sustains your life and practice. Use it as your guide.

Q. Don't you think that the harsh practice in some Japanese monasteries is a kind of group superego?

R. It's the dark side of Zen Buddhism and I'm sorry about it. You know, properly integrated, some seemingly harsh practice can be helpful and encouraging. It can be very good. But I feel generally that just sitting is difficult enough. There was a woman at an early sesshin who was literally vaulting over people who were sitting in zazen in order to get to dokusan. She was carrying on from the practice at another far more demanding center.

Q. Did you tell her to cool out?

R. Yes, I certainly did and she settled down.

Q. That's the dark side. We hear so many stories of Japanese monks sitting with chin rests, hanging on to a rope to stay awake, pushing themselves.

R. Part of it is cultural. That's all right. Part of it is extreme and is open to criticism even in Japan. I did my first Japanese sesshin at Engaku-ji, which is the monastery where Nyogen Senzaki and D. T. Suzuki trained. I had read in *The Training of the Zen Buddhist Monk* how head monks pull people off the *tan* and drag them into dokusan, but seeing it happen was a lot more vivid than reading about it.[7] At Engaku-ji the rōshi's residence is at the foot of the garden. You walk through the garden to the dokusan line in the entryway to the house. When it's your turn, you walk completely through the house to his room in the back. At the first dokusan of the sesshin I attended, a young monk remained on his cushions and wouldn't go. So he was hauled off the *tan* by two or three senior monks. He grasped everything to keep from going. Zoris were flying and there was a lot of shouting. The senior monks got him through the door of the zendō and into the garden, but he broke away and waded into the lily pond and sat down in zazen on the island in the middle of the pond. So the monks had to wade out to the little island to drag him to the dokusan room—where he got a poor reception, I imagine.

You know what *shibai* means? A big act. That's what I thought it was. A big act. The monk acts as though he were in deep Samādhi and doesn't want to be disturbed. So the head monks act as if they know that this is the very time he should see the rōshi and should be forced. Nonsense. There are plenty of monasteries where the procedure is more natural. People know that when it's time for dokusan, you can go if you wish. If the rōshi wants to see a particular monk who is still in the zendō, the head monk will tap the monk and say, "Rōshi wants to see you." So the monk will gasshō, get up and go. No monkey business. The *shibai* turns Zen practice into a cult: "I'm tough, I endured all this. Others endured it too. We're tough." And so you and your Sangha become something special and something arrogant.

Q. So have we inherited not only our own superego but also some other culture's superego on top of it?

R. So it seems. It behooves us to be discriminating.

Q. The American superego, I think, is mostly valuative, critical. In the taxonomy we use in our education course, the valuative processes are rated as the top, above the synthesis, which is the creative process. We're all being pushed to be critical from the word go. The Asian way seems to push toward something else.

R. Yes, toward the next cognition, perhaps. As Zen students we are creatures of two cultures so we can stand aside from them both and take the best of each.

Q. I think we tend to be judgmental about our Asian ancestors and colleagues. It all comes back to Dōgen's question about why it is necessary to sweat blood in order to prove something that is already true.

R. Yes, and Dōgen's question relates to our own practice in the West. By the fact that we are not professional monks and nuns, we tend to set forth too easy a path.

Q. Would you say our practice is easy?

R. No, our scheduling is too easy. We don't pay enough attention to the importance of sitting regularly, night and morning. But generally lay practice is a dilemma. We are still working it out. Thinking back to the old days at the Maui Zendō—we sat together, twenty or twenty-five people, morning, noon, and evening, with work periods in between, five days a week, then had zazen-kai every weekend. It was great.

But there was a problem. When people left the Maui Zendō

they went through serious reentry difficulties. They were often angry and couldn't say why they were angry. Looking back, I can see that our schedule was, in a sense, quite artificial. We can't do it that way anymore. The culture has shifted. The late 1960s and early 1970s were an exceptional time that is not likely to come again. Now we have to fold practice into our ordinary lives.

Q. Dōgen talks about sincerity, about being thoroughgoing in one's practice. He also says when one is not full of the Dharma one feels that it is complete, when one is full of the Dharma something seems to be lacking.

R. When you think you are complete, there is something lacking in your body and mind. When you know there is something missing, you are complete. That's an awareness of "not yet, not enough, not enough yet."

Q. So zeal is moment-by-moment discovering "not enough"?

R. Yes. It works for sincerity too. You can be thinking, "I'm not sincere enough." If you take this as a teaching and don't brood on it, then such discovery can be a buoy, a beacon. Zeal and sincerity are interesting because they have so many overtones.

Q. Most religious wars have zeal as a motive; how do you work with misguided zeal?

R. How do you work with the Yugoslavian war right now? Is there a way that you can put yourself between the factions as peace groups did during the war in Nicaragua, stepping into the zone between the Sandinistas and the Contras? What do you feel about this?

Q. Well, I suppose that one could try to find the traditions of tolerance, which there surely must be on each side. In Buddhism there are virtues like the Four Noble Abodes that can dissolve misguided zeal.[8] I am sure that one can find such virtues in the two traditions of the former Yugoslavia: Orthodox Christianity and Islam. It would be a matter of searching them out and making a point of them.

R. You are right about Buddhism and about other religions. Such virtues are perennially human and simply take one form here and another there. But making a point of those perennial virtues on the ground of the conflict would take a lot of zeal, wouldn't it!

Q. I'd like to go back to zeal itself. Can we connect it with a certain goal?

R. You know, this whole matter of goals is an important one for the peace worker or the Zen student. I think that it's important to have a goal. But how specific is that goal? Are you seduced by your goal, bathing in fantasies about it? That's where the goal is no good. But outright denial of purpose can also be misleading. When I worked with Senzaki Sensei, he would tell us, "Don't think about realization." So I just put it out of my mind completely. I just sat there without any particular theme, my mind busy with thoughts. I misunderstood him, I'm sure. We didn't have the ground for understanding him in those days. You need a clear practice and a trust that the practice is the goal, that peace is the way. But in those early days we didn't even recite the *Heart Sūtra*. We had never heard of Hakuin Zenji.

You really need some resolve like that of Brother Lawrence: "Even if it takes me all the rest of this year, even if it takes ten years, even if it takes me the rest of my life." Take up some kind of vow like that. Do you call it a goal? If you do, then that's fine—it's a wonderful goal.

Q. Doesn't that keep many people from what they are supposed to do? I mean, they cling to the idea, "I have to reach it. I have to do it. I have to make it."

R. No, no. I'm not saying "I have to reach it, I have to make it." I'm saying, "Even if it takes me all the rest of my life I'm just going to do *Mu.*" I'm not setting a specific goal of realization for myself.

Q. You have mentioned that every step is the goal.

R. Yes, that's right. That's the interesting thing about these Pāramitās. There is not a progression from Dāna to Shīla, Kshānti, Vīrya, Dhyāna, Prajñā. It's not step by step, but each one perfected is the perfection, so to speak. That's especially interesting when you look at "reaching the other shore" as the interpretation of Pāramitā. In other words, to reach Nirvāna. The perfection of any of them is Nirvāna.

Q. What is Nirvāna?

R. The archetype of Kuan-yin exemplifies it. Those of you who have visited the Honolulu Academy of Arts know the figure of Kuan-yin. She is a kind of symbol of the Academy too—one of their first acquisitions. When I was a twelve-year-old boy, I used to go to the Academy to see her when she was the only figure in the Asian room that is now filled with other exhibits. She was seated on the low dais, just where she is now, but the rest of the room was completely empty—with some benches where we could sit and enjoy her. She sits like this [demonstrates with an arm across an upraised knee] in the Mudrā of Royal Ease. Surely that is Nirvāna. She is our ideal, enjoying the sounds of the world. But our practice of asking "Who is hearing?" is also Royal Ease.

Q. During the last sesshin I attended on the East Coast they broke five sticks across the backs of people doing zazen. That makes me think about Royal Ease. It seems there was an awful lot of pushing and yet I didn't see any kind of understanding there. Here it doesn't seem like there's an awful lot of pushing, yet I see a kind of understanding.

R. There's no need to beat people. Kuan-yin is a better model—or Pu-tai, a figure for Maitreya, the future Buddha, who practices in the marketplace. He has a bag full of the candy and the toys that he gives to children. That is his practice and he works at it. But what a pleasant, easy practice it is!

Q. Doesn't ease come from practice? I mean, it's like when you begin to drive a car. You have to work hard to learn. But when you practice it and practice it, then ease comes.

R. Yes. At the same time we have the negative model of the person who works very hard and suddenly retires and can't handle it. There must be that element of ease throughout one's life. In fact, you can't learn how to drive a car without it.

Q. Would you say Flora Courtois was just born with Vīrya? Didn't she have to ask herself anything?

R. She did ask herself something. Her life story is extremely interesting. Her very early memories are of rescuing spiders in the house and escorting them outside, rescuing insects in the pond to keep them from drowning and this kind of thing. Then puberty hit her like a ton of bricks. She hadn't been socializing during her early childhood, I guess. She couldn't just suddenly socialize and she was plunged into misery. She had an idyllic childhood where she felt one with nature and then as an adolescent she felt completely cut off and anxious. She didn't put it into words this way, but when she reached puberty she was anxious for the original garden. So her motive, her incentive was "What is it that underlies everything?" This was what she was trying to understand. There are a lot of teenagers with this question, but not all of them can follow through. There are also a lot of eight-year-olds out there rescuing little frogs in front of the mowers.

Q. Rōshi, I might believe that certain Buddhist practices or Buddhist studies support Vīrya. But how should I practice in an intentional community that includes people who don't have the same beliefs, who are not convinced that study and purposeful practice are that important, who don't see themselves as Buddhists? How can I implement these practices without alienating people who don't accept their importance?

R. Well, it seems to me there are two points here. The first is that an intentional community is one that is intentionally formed. Its members are intentionally chosen. If you choose people who are not like-minded, then you work with who you have, taking all the needs and views of the folks into consideration and synthesizing that as a community.

The second point is that even in communities that are entirely Buddhist, you can have divisions. There are a large number of Buddhist meditation groups scattered around the country that are formed of people who have moved to a particular place and have various kinds of backgrounds. These might include Vajrayāna people and Vipassanā people, people from Sasaki Rōshi's dōjō, people from Rochester, and so on. How do you make a community out of such folks? It seems to me you have to find the common denominator. Eventually if the community evolves, it's likely to split. There are people who are naturally Vipassanā and there are people who are naturally Zen. As these folks become more and more conscious of their true motives, natural divisions will evolve.

Q. Is there natural zazen and natural Vipassanā, but no natural Shākyamuni?

R. No, I'm not saying there is natural zazen or natural Vipassanā. It is just that one has an affinity for zazen or one has an affinity for mindfulness practice. One of the first things that Mr. Blyth, my first Zen friend, said to me (using the sexist language of the 1940s), "There's a man for every religion and a religion for every man." We need to honor this diversity

Q. To return to Vīrya and community, I take part in a meditation group in northern California that includes people from very different places. How can we find common forms that support and encourage Vīrya?

R. One bell at the beginning and one bell at the end. [Laughter] But even in a small group like yours, affinity groups will naturally evolve within the Sangha and this can be the beginning of growth and division, which can be very healthy.

Q. I've been sitting here musing about purpose. I don't think I am so concerned about enlightenment. Maybe my purpose is just to be happy and not suffer so much. Maybe it's just something really corny like just trying to exist in this world without creating more hassles or something. That's what I get down to sometimes.

R. I don't think there's anything wrong with that. The Buddha was talking about that, wasn't he? That was his point about Duhkha, about anguish. There is a release from Duhkha but it's not something that happens with one milestone. There is milestone after milestone.

FIVE

SETTLED, FOCUSED MEDITATION

The Dhyāna Pāramitā

With the Dhyāna Pāramitā we move from the realm of morality into absorption, meditation, concentration—the realm of Samādhi. The two words *Dhyāna* and *Samādhi* are used almost interchangeably, particularly in East Asia, where they are sometimes combined into a single term.[1] However, they can and should be distinguished. In formal practice, Dhyāna is the form and method of zazen and Samādhi is its condition.

As the form and method, Dhyāna is charged with powerful implications. It is the archetypal Buddha seated under the Bodhi tree. It is also the method of settled, focused meditation he used and it is the method we use in our centers today.

Zen Buddhism is, etymologically at least, the inheritor of the Dhyāna tradition, for the name *Zen* derives through transliteration from the Chinese *Ch'an,* abbreviated from *Ch'an-na,* which comes in turn from Dhyāna. The extraordinary thing is that although Dhyāna is the name of our sect and is our primary method, usually not much instruction is given about it beyond advice to sit with the back straight, the spine bent forward slightly at the waistline, ears on a line with the shoulders, and nose on a line with the navel. Count your breaths, we are told. Within these very broad guidelines, the student has to reinvent the Way.

There are certain advantages to reinvention. Once mastered, it is never lost. But lots of time can be wasted in exploring bypaths. I prefer to teach the perfection of zazen as I understand it, in as much detail as possible.

For all the explanation, however, it is a simple method. Senzaki Nyogen Sensei often quoted his teacher, Shaku Sōen Zenji: "Zazen is not a difficult task. It is a way to lead you to your long-lost home."[2] It doesn't take much time to find that home. In fact, if you lower your eyes and breathe quietly in and out, your distractions disappear and your long-lost home is right there. Notice what a pleasant place it is! How free you are—not tugged back and forth by contending thoughts, not pushed around by the voice of your conscience saying, "It's not good! You're no good! You're not doing it!" Everything is quiet; everything is peaceful. Suzuki Shunryū Rōshi used to say, "When you follow your breaths, you are like a swinging door. Nothing comes in, nothing goes out."[3] This is your original dwelling place.

There are many references to this original home in Zen Buddhist literature. In Case 42 of *The Gateless Barrier* we read:

> *Once Mañjushrī went to a place where many Buddhas had assembled with the World Honored One. When he arrived, he found that all of them had returned to their original dwelling place.*[4]

Where is the original dwelling place of the many Buddhas? Home thus becomes a kōan, but it needn't. It can be just a matter of taking a bath:

> *In the old days there were sixteen Bodhisattvas who entered their bath together at their usual time. All of them realized the causation of water and cried out with one voice, "The essence of touch is subtle and clear! We have attained the place where the sons and daughters of the Buddha dwell!"*[5]

Bodhidharma at home is also a central archetype. After he had his unsatisfactory audience with the Emperor of Liang, he journeyed to the Kingdom of Wei in the northwestern part of China. He found a ruined temple with a cave behind it that was just right for his zazen and in time four disciples came and sat with him. Meantime, the Emperor's religious advisor asked:

"Your Majesty, do you know who that was?"

The Emperor said, "I don't know."

The Advisor said, "That was the Great Personage Kuan-yin bearing the mind seal of the Buddha." The Emperor was regretful and sought to have a messenger dispatched to invite Bodhidharma to return.

The Advisor said, "Even if you send everyone in China after him, he will not come back."[6]

No, you had your chance, Your Majesty. He has gone to his true home and will never ever leave there.

Sitting quietly, facing the wall like Bodhidharma, as Bodhidharma, is the vast and fathomless Dharma itself. It is the home of practice. But explaining the original dwelling place in such a way can be like showing a rose to a new gardener. How to get from here to there is the question.

In the days when the National Teacher Hui-chung held forth in the capital of China, it was said that no monk's training was complete—no monk was truly secure in his true home—until he had paid his respects to the old master. Nan-ch'üan and two brother monks set out see him.

Halfway there, Nan-ch'üan drew a circle on the ground and said, "If you can say something, then let's go on." Kuei-tsung seated himself inside the circle and Ma-ku made a woman's bow before him.

Nan-ch'üan said, "Then let's not go on."

Kuei-tsung said, "What's going on in your mind?"[7]

The three brothers, out to find their true home, were practicing Dhyāna, pursuing the Dharma with all their hearts. It turns out that they already were there, halfway along on their pilgrimage. Nan-ch'üan built the floor and walls, and the other two completed the job. When Kuei-tsung said, "What's going on in your mind?" what was going on in his? I'll leave that for you to muse on.

When you settle in your own circle, you find no coming or going, no problem with importunate thoughts. Easier said than done. Our great Ancestors were, you can be sure, victims of the same tapes of incessant thinking that trouble the rest of us: loops of paranoia, sex, and acclamation that are so persistent and tiresome. How did they handle this dilemma?

They started where they were, just as you and I must start where we are. Our breath is our home, not just provisionally, but throughout our practice and our lives. Count your breaths from one to ten. Settle into each point in the sequence so that everything else is quiet. There is only one, only two, only three, in the whole world. To be sure, you are taking up a sequence, but the act of counting is to become intimate with each point—just one, just two, just three. You are intimate with each point of no dimension, as Kuei-tsung found intimacy with the exact center of the universe.

There at the center your loop of thoughts dies down. You are formed by sounds and sights and smells. Sounds, sights, and smells inform you, for if you stray a bit from the center they prompt you to return. This is the ground of all action and is not anti-intellectual. Our great Ancestors, beginning with the Buddha himself, had magnificent intellects and used their minds cogently and vigorously in their teachings. But first things first. Your practice is to cut off the loops. However, your thoughts will not die down if you try to block them. The more you press against them, the more they press against you. This pressing is a single act. It is you pressing you and the upshot is that you get tired and frustrated.

Some teachers try to induce this dilemma. Their rationale is that when students feel blocked on every side, they will finally turn about and break through the loop once and for all. I feel doubtful about this. It seems to postulate a leap from ordinary being to Buddhahood. Is there really a Buddha apart from ordinary being? Yet if trying to beat Buddhahood into a hapless student does not seem appropriate, what would be the correct method?

To begin with, thoughts tend to come and go like waves on the sea, sometimes overwhelming thoughts, very threatening thoughts.

Luo-shan asked Yen-t'ou, "What about when thoughts come and go without ceasing?"

Yen-t'ou scolded him, saying, "Who comes and goes?"[8]

Who indeed! As Chao-chou says, the true Buddha is sitting in the house.[9] Does that this mean that by zazen one can somehow cut through contending thoughts and become that true Buddha?

Ma-tsu sat in the Zen hall every day, all day long. Nan-yüeh asked him, "What is your purpose in meditating?"

Ma-tsu said, "I wish to become a Buddha."

Nan-yüeh took a piece of roofing tile and began rubbing it with a stone. Ma-tsu asked, "What are you doing?"

Nan-yüeh said, "I am polishing it to make a mirror."

Ma-tsu said, "How can you make a mirror by polishing a piece of tile?"

Nan-yüeh said, "Granted. How can you become a Buddha by sitting in meditation?"

Ma-tsu said, "Then what would be right?"

Nan-yüeh said, "It is like an ox pulling a cart. If the cart does not go, do you hit the cart or the ox?"[10]

This case is the classic lesson in the vanity of anticipation and of the unity of method and result that I come back to again and again.[11] Dōgen Zenji clarifies the inner teaching of the story in his inimitable way:

> *Indeed we know that when a tile, as it is being polished, becomes a mirror, Ma-tsu becomes a Buddha. When Ma-tsu becomes a Buddha, Ma-tsu becomes Ma-tsu instantly. When Ma-tsu becomes Ma-tsu, zazen becomes zazen instantly. Therefore, the tradition of making a mirror by polishing a tile has been kept alive in the core of ancient Buddhas.*[12]

Hee-Jin Kim in turn clarifies Dōgen's apparent contradiction of Nan-yüeh:

> *The tile is not transformed into the mirror, but the tile* is *the mirror; the act of polishing the tile itself is to unfold the purity of the mirror. Consequently, zazen, likened to the act of polishing the tile in this case, is nothing other than the unfolding enactment of original enlightenment, that is, the mirror. At one level, Dōgen affirms the conventional interpretation of the story, but at another, he penetrates the matter far more deeply so that the story is now seen to have an entirely new significance. The real issue is not whether to meditate, but how to meditate; the* how *is obviously not a matter of technique so much as a matter of authenticity.*[13]

Authenticity is the key, but it is not a problem. If you are sincere enough to come here and give it a go, that is enough to start with. Sincerity builds. Authenticity builds. Character builds. How do they build? Like everything else—with practice.

Practice is not just a matter of formal zazen. In Zen Buddhist schools, we tend to think of Dhyāna practice as the way of rigorous zazen, exacting dokusan or interviews, and cogent teishōs or Dharma talks. But Dhyāna is also a matter of character, specifically spelled out in the old texts as the Brahma-vihāras, the Four Noble Abodes of loving kindness, compassion, joy in the liberation of others, and equanimity or impartiality.[14] Hakuin Zenji agrees:

> *Offerings, precepts, Pāramitās*
> Nembutsu, *atonement, practice—*
> *the many other virtues—*
> *all rise within zazen.*[15]

They rise within there because zazen is the practice of dropping away body and mind, of completely forgetting the self and its preoccupations. The forgotten self is the unselfish self, at one with the self of all beings across the world and back through time, as all our rituals remind us.

This ultimate forgetting is the Great Death, which brings forth the Great Life. Without such transition and its practice, Zen or any form of Buddhism is just a cultist trick, as we have seen to our pain in the past, continuing even into the present. It is inspiring for me as a Zen Buddhist to recall that the very name of my way of life implies compassion and equanimity as well as allowing my body and mind to drop away in formal zazen. It is essential that we find rituals of unselfish loving-kindness, compassion, joy in the liberation of others, and equanimity. It is essential that we formulate skillful means for applying these ideals and then actually apply them.

The Four Noble Abodes are lofty halls of this very life of family, workplace, and Sangha, but Dhyāna, the practice of dropping away body and mind, is rununciation. Here again the model is the Buddha under the Bodhi tree. For the Buddha, renunciation meant leaving his wife and son to seek his spiritual fortune as a monk. Har Dayal quotes an early Buddhist text that dismisses the Buddha's marriage as a romantic episode.[16] That should ruffle your feathers! I am a husband and father and almost all Western Buddhists likewise are householders. The model of the Buddha's renunciation can't be literal for us, obviously. There is little or no place for the Sannyāsin, the wandering mendicant, in our culture. Even the priests at our large Buddhist centers in the West are married for the most part and have families. Our renunciation is not that of the Buddha, but it is the Buddha's renunciation nonetheless, for religious practice is austere; it involves giving up many things and not just because we don't have time for them. As householders, our renunciation is a certain lifestyle that we follow together with spouse, children, and friends. It may involve retreats, but more generally it is the effort to live the simple way of integrity and honor.

QUESTIONS AND RESPONSES

Q. How do you see the method of shikantaza as taught by Suzuki Shunryū Rōshi and the method of *Mu* as taught in our school? Can you see big differences there? Do the same outcomes and experiences come from both schools?

R. The same experience will sometimes emerge. Let me say that I think there are kōan people and there are shikantaza people. I respect both ways and both kinds of people and can teach both. Because I myself am oriented toward kōan study, I tend to attract kōan-oriented people. But some shikantaza people do come and just ignore all the talk about kōans, which is fine.

Actually, there is something missing in both ways. The path of kōan study tends to miss the richness of zazen itself. People who take up shikantaza and practice it with the utmost rigor inevitably cultivate character change by the fact that in their meditation they are scrupulously honest at the very source of thoughts. They don't indulge in self-preoccupation at all. This honesty carries through into daily life. At the same time, an inquiring spirit is not especially encouraged in their practice. Thus, they may not address the vital question of life and death—and for some people that's all right. The student of kōans, on the other hand, is likely, unless cautioned and helped, to devote a kind of intellectual energy to kōan study. There is no true settling as a result. The original dwelling place is rather neglected.

One can see all this in the faces of old-time students. A Rinzai person might have a deep metaphysical understanding but without any real peace. The Sōtō person might have found a certain level of peace but without any real understanding. I would like to follow the best of each way.

Q. These distinctions of Sōtō and Rinzai weren't so clear in early Zen, were they?

R. No. At the time of Tung-shan or Lin-chi there wasn't any sectarian distinction. But little differences were already discernible. The two disciples of the Sixth Ancestor were Nan-yüeh and Ch'ing-yüan. It's from these two that separate streams eventually emerged. There's the story about San-sheng and Hsüeh-feng: San-sheng was a disciple of Lin-chi—on the Nan-yüeh side. Hsüeh-feng was on the other side of the transmission chart—descended from Ch'ing-yüan. Anyway, San-sheng came to Hsüeh-feng, who was very old at this time. San-sheng was in his forties. He had just completed his formal study and was full of self-confidence. He asked, "When 'golden scales' has passed through the net, I wonder what should he eat?" There is a bit of interchange about this. Finally, Hsüeh-feng said, "I'm sorry. This old monk is too busy with temple affairs to attend to you." He had nothing to prove at all.[17] So you can see very different styles even early on. But of course even today, you can find tough-minded, aggressive Sōtō people and very mild, modest Rinzai people.

Q. Didn't Yasutani Rōshi and also Yamada Rōshi recommend shikantaza after finishing kōan practice? I'm wondering if that's the way to reach the balance.

R. Yes. They suggested that shikantaza is one mode of practice you can take up after you finish kōan study. I myself work on *Mu.* The only time that Yamada Rōshi talked to me about his own practice after finishing his kōan study, he said, "I work on Bassui Zenji's kōan, 'Who is hearing that sound?' " So for those people who have finished kōan study, I suggest that they experiment. Usually, however, by that time they already know what they want to do.

Q. How can one find peace when doing kōan study?

R. Really, it isn't that different from shikantaza. You don't sit there on your cushions and stare at a complicated kōan like "Mañjushrī and the Young Woman in Samādhi." If you do, it just goes around and around in your head. It's best to memorize the kōan, pick out what you think might be the first point, reduce it to its most succinct formulation, and then stare at that. One of the most talented students of kōan study I've ever met, not one of my own students, said to me, "I don't work on my kōan in the dōjō. I count my breaths. When I get in line to see the rōshi, I don't work on my kōan. When I'm walking down the hall to see him, I'm still counting my breaths. And then finally after I sit up from my bows before the rōshi, I recite my kōan and examine it with him." That's confidence!

Q. Some teachers now are using the personal problems of students as kōans. What do you think of that?

R. I have suggested that a dilemma in daily life be treated as a kōan, that is, you can contain the problem, focus upon it, and allow its solution to emerge. Strictly speaking, however, the kōan is a story from old texts upon which you concentrate on your cushions. It has proved itself empirically over the ages to be a succinct presentation of some aspect of the particular, the universal, and their harmony. This is the arena of formal Zen

Buddhist study. So if a student comes to me with a personal problem, my practice is to suggest quieting the mind with regular zazen so that options will become clearer. If the problem is pressing and I sense that a lifetime neurosis is involved, I will commonly refer the student to a psychotherapist.

Q. I have heard that it is possible for people with lifetime neuroses to pass kōans and become teachers.

R. That's a different matter. We can appreciate Nan-ch'üan giving Chao-chou one look when Chao-chou was eighteen and saying, "Ah, there's a good one." Yet Chao-chou went on to live with Nan-ch'üan for another forty years, polishing his wisdom and compassion. That is the genuine path. Chao-chou did not have a mere knack for passing kōans. He did not fall into the lazy way of responding just on the basis of his initial insight. It is very important that the teacher and the student both zero in on keeping the Great Matter intimate and personal—and then applying it wherever possible. If the teacher does not insist on this and the successors go out and teach and fail, then the Ancestors are betrayed.

Q. You quoted Yamada Rōshi once, saying that these people who abuse their position of trust cast a shadow on the completeness of their realization.

R. Yamada Rōshi did say that, but they are words that need to be explicated. Surely he is not talking about the peak experience all by itself. He is also talking about the cultivation of that experience before and after—and the constant work of applying the implications of insight in daily life. He is talking about the background study for kōan work, the Precepts and Pāramitās and the Four Abodes, and other useful schemes—and all the care that is necessary to tie them metaphysically and morally to everyday conduct. Discussing this with Brother David Steindl-Rast recently, I confessed that one of the reasons I felt powerless to speak about some of these egregious incidents of Zen teachers exploiting their students was that I didn't understand them. How could this happen? One involved a person who had been wise and compassionate in guiding me as a friend. So we're not talking about something linear or black and white here. It's a very complex matter. Character perfection is very important and we must seek every possible means to effect it. I think I've strayed from your question.

Q. No. This is to the point, but I feel that when someone authenticates someone else as a teacher, it implies that there has been some character transformation. We have our old stories of a person staying with a teacher for forty years or living under a bridge for ten or fifteen years; a long process of maturation is involved here regardless of when a person has a great insight. We don't have that so much now. There's a need for teachers, so our teachers are often younger. But they're authenticated. A student realizes there are dangers in going to somebody who sets up on a street corner or just flies over from India. But with someone in a lineage, there's a sense that this person has somehow been authenticated.

R. When we look at those teachers from Japan who have not done well, we find that some of them left rather early and didn't spend many years with their teachers.

Q. You have shown how Dhyāna includes the Four Noble Abodes. Does it include Right Mindfulness and other elements of Classical Buddhism? How about the Eightfold Path? How about Right Mindfulness?

R. Yes, Dhyāna does include Right Mindfulness, though I prefer the translation "Right Recollection." *Mindfulness* implies the practice of noticing what you are doing; heel, foot, ball, toe as you walk, for example. That can be an aid to concentration, perhaps, but it doesn't go very deep and it doesn't involve anyone or anything except the empirical self.

In rendering the term *Right Recollection* we move from the empirical self to Zen Buddhism and to Mahāyāna practice generally. The term *Nembutsu,* which is usually translated "Calling the Name of the Buddha," can be translated "Recalling Buddha" or "Remembering Buddha." As a Zen Buddhist, I regard

Just A Note

The other book is "The Wandering Taoist," published I think in the 1980s; written by this man's disciple — a Chinese name I can't remember. Will try to find more exact information.

Wonderful talking to you this morning. Your call came in when G. was on the phone to his stockbroker — the phone signals and identifies "incoming call" on the screen. So G. knew to call you back.

Much love,
Dorothy

the *Nembutsu* as a recollection of the Buddha as my true home. The first of the Three Vows of Refuge is really a *Nembutsu,* "I return to the Buddha as my true home." The other two Vows of Refuge are also Right Recollection: "I return to the Dharma as my true home; I return to the Sangha as my true home." Recalling these vows is Right Recollection in daily life. Remembering your true home when you first sit down on your cushions is Right Recollection in the dōjō. Chao-chou's words can be helpful:

> *A monk asked Chao-chou, "How should I use the twenty-four hours?"*
>
> *Chao-chou said, "You are used by the twenty-four hours. I use the twenty-four hours."*[18]

Use your time! Zazen is for zazen! The pernicious temptation—"Oh, now this important topic has come up in my mind and I had better resolve it before I go back to my zazen"—this must be cut off and the topic set aside for later.

This cutting off does not involve muscular effort. It is a matter simply of returning to the comfortable, joyous place where nothing is happening. There are plenty of times when thoughts are important and useful but keep your sense of proportion. Right Recollection is the practice of perfection. Then thoughts serve you. Thoughts sustain you. Thoughts nurture you, bring sustenance to you.

Q. Isn't it perfectly natural for thoughts to arise in one's mind?

R. The *Emmei Jikku Kannon Gyō* says, "Rapidly thoughts arise in the mind, thought after thought is not separate from mind."[19] This is a natural mechanism. Perhaps that is not a good word—thoughts are not "mechanisms." They are the universe coming forth in the mind just as it comes forth in the cry of the gecko or in the shining of the leaves. Dealing with thoughts is not a tug of war.

Still, most Zen Buddhist teachers use martial metaphors. I have sat in many sesshins in Japan where the rōshi comes in at the end of the first evening and says, "Now we are gathering for the battle." On the second night he comes in and says, "Now we can see the enemy," and so on. By the fourth day we're fighting hand to hand!

That's not necessary. Just take one long *Mu* sigh, "*Muuuuu.*" I tell people in the dokusan room that the sigh is not just Zen practice but is really grandmother wisdom. Our grandmothers knew that when they sighed deliberately the pressure they felt tended to ease. And what is tension but pressure of thought!

Q. It seems to me that Right Recollection involves memory. Isn't that the thinking mind?

R. I don't know. Memory is very mysterious. Physiologists of the brain aren't able to locate the seat of memory exactly. Some are suggesting that every cell is the seat of memory. Everything that has ever happened is encoded in every cell in existence, not only in the human brain, not only in the human body, but in every cell of every being, including animals and plants. If this is correct, then memory is more accessible to human beings than it is to others, probably because language is such a convenient mechanism for it. There's that word again.

Q. I still don't see how memory can be part of Dhyāna. You say we should recall Buddha as our refuge and home when we first sit down to zazen. Does memory have a role in the zazen after the first few minutes of formal practice?

R. Sure. When you allow yourself to be open to the Buddha as your home, as yourself really, then you are tuned in such a way throughout your zazen. You are Shākyamuni regardless of gender. You sit there, rooted to the center of the earth. You bring the chaos of undifferentiation into your human body and extend it above the heavens as a distinctly unique Tathāgata. You are walking hand in hand with all the Ancestors, the hair of your eyebrows entangled with theirs. True memory dissolves time. Right Recollection brings all Ancestors to this room. Or, rather, it reminds us that they have been here all along.

Q. Is it possible to practice without them?

R. Of course! Begin with posture and counting your breaths.

Q. I have heard mention of *Shikan-Mu.* Is that what you're getting at?

R. One of my Zen friends uses this term. It's an instructive one. Dōgen Zenji used *shikan* to mean "body and mind fallen away." *Shikan-Mu* is pure *Mu* standing forth with nothing sticking to it. Without using that particular expression, this is what I teach. People come to me and say, "I don't think that I am giving enough inquiry to my *Mu.*" And so I say, "Please don't worry about it. Your natural anxiety to understand is your method. So just breathe *Mu* quietly. Settle into *Mu.*"

Q. If everybody's path is his or her own path, how do you reconcile that with saying that if you're going to take this path, you've got to do it this way?

R. I offer guidelines to help keep people on track.

Q. I thought that my way is different from anybody else's way.

R. In detail, certainly. But, for example, I will suggest that you count your breaths, inhalation and exhalation. And then you try exhalation only. And then you try inhalation only. Then you try following the breaths, and then shikantaza. Which way is best for you? What is your purpose? So in a general way, then, I can put together what is likely to be the best path for you. If you say your purpose is realizing your true nature, understanding who you are, coping with death, or something like that, then I'll put you on a kōan track. If you're on a kōan track, you're going to have to count your breaths one of those three ways when you first sit down, until your mind is reasonably quiet. And then you're going to have to settle into *Mu,* and you're going to have to know what *Mu* is. There are one or two alternate possibilities if you don't relate to *Mu.*

There's even the option for a person who is Christian and finds foreign words unappealing. In such a case, I say, " 'In the beginning was the word'—what is that word?" So there are a number of different possibilities—but not nearly as many possibilities as there are people or religious paths. If a person comes from a Vipassanā center, say, and is very strict about wanting just to watch thoughts, tag them, and let them go, then I am obliged to say that I can't be the teacher. I don't have the expertise. Such a person is welcome to come here to any of our meetings, but if that person wants to come to sesshin, I'm not so happy about it because people in sesshin come to dokusan, and what am I going to do in dokusan with this person?

Q. You're suggesting then that different paths apply to, or create, or nurture different modes of consciousness?

R. You bet. The goal is different and the understanding that comes out of it is different. The differences too are different. Vipassanā and Transcendental Meditation are excellent foundations for Zen practice and I'm sure Zen practice is an excellent foundation for them, but there are some practices that are not a good foundation for Zen. Kundalini Yoga, for example. You must unlearn Kundalini to do Zen—and vice versa.

Q. Would we be wise to turn our attention and energy inward and avoid outside distractions?

R. Inevitably you will find that the outside synchronizes with the inside. Excessive distractions appear for excessively distracted people. As you go along in your practice you find that outside things are actually teachings. Let me give you an example. It's a kind of intellectual example but it's a good one. I have been thinking a lot lately about how perception works—how perception feeds the self, how it is the self. In the course of wandering around the bookstore at the University of California at Davis, I picked up a new William James reader, published by the State University of New York. I thought, "Oh, this looks interesting," so I bought it and put it in my bag. I came home and I looked at James and was fascinated because he seemed to be speaking to the very things I was groping for. And then, lo and behold, here's David Kalupahana's book, *Principles of Buddhist Psychology,* which he links to William James.[20] Those things I was reading in James that were speaking to my particular interest suddenly became much clearer. Kalupahana is a professional philosopher who knows his field inside and out, so he selected passages from Buddhism and from James and showed how they were saying the same thing—particularly that there is no agent of perception. A person who was not interested in that particular theme might walk right by James in the bookstore. Such a person also might not so readily pick up Kalupahana but would be following other things, another theme or maybe just the static of popular culture. As you settle in your practice and find a particular path, then all things come to you.

Q. Rōshi, when you say there's no agent of perception, do you mean there's no continuous agent of perception?

R. There's no fixed agent of perception. The self is unique all right, but so is each river. Some people come to me in the dokusan room and say, "I want to know who is doing *Mu.*" So I say, "Who is asking, 'Who is doing *Mu*?' " The cat is chasing its tail. As soon as you ask, it changes. The self is a particular flow sustained by the gecko, by conversations with friends, by reading, by eating, by sleeping.

Q. What is unique about my particular flow?

R. Little nose.

SIX

WISDOM

The Prajñā Pāramitā

The Sixth Pāramitā is Prajñā, the raison d'être of the Buddha Way. If Dāna is the entry to the Dharma, then Prajñā is its realization and the other Pāramitās are Prajñā in alternate forms.

The philosophical and psychological understanding of Prajñā is illumination that arises in the human mind. Zen Buddhist teachers don't talk about it very much. For example, according to the traditional story, when the young monk Hui-neng came to Hung-jen for the first time, he said, "May I tell Your Holiness that Prajñā frequently arises in my mind?"[1] Hung-jen changed the subject and sent him to the backyard to hull the rice.

Later in his own teaching, Hui-neng did speak of Prajñā, but linked it with Dhyāna, likening Prajñā to the light and Dhyāna to the lamp.[2] Without the practice of settled, focused meditation, realization is not possible. And without realization, the practice is dark.

You will find acknowledgment of the philosophical and the psychological implications of Prajñā in Zen Buddhist commentaries, but there is more to Prajñā, far more. I remember how I puzzled over the remark by a Zen Buddhist friend when I was still young in my practice. We were speaking of Prajñā and he said, "The song of birds is Prajñā; the sound of the wind is Prajñā." I didn't understand; it didn't make sense. But as my father used to say when I found something that had been there all along, "If it had been a bear it would have bitten you." The old teachers used a snake metaphor instead:

Hsüeh-feng said to his assembly, "On this South Mountain, there is a turtle-nosed snake. You should all watch out for it."

His disciples then point out that lots of people have been bitten to death, and question why he just said "South Mountain."[3] Speaking of that same snake, Ch'ing-lin said there's nowhere to escape it, but the grass is so deep that we can't find it.[4] That's the problem. As the Buddha said, our delusions and preoccupations obscure the living fact.

Yet for all its importance, Prajñā appears only once by name in our kōan study:

A monk asked Chih-men, "What is the essence of Prajñā?"
Chih-men said, "The oyster encloses the bright moon."
The monk asked, "What is the function of Prajñā?"
Chih-men said, "The rabbit conceives her young."[5]

Chih-men couches his replies in terms of Chinese folklore about how pearls are formed and rabbits are conceived by the light of the full moon. In working on this case recently, a student remarked that it gave him a sense of the ancient, of the timeless. Indeed, Prajñā is the timeless in circumstances of time. But that is saying much more than Chih-men intended.

Dōgen Zenji mentions Prajñā in his essay on practice called *Bendōwa*, "Endeavor of the Way," but only in the phrase "the seed of Prajñā," the Prajñā potential everyone shares and must cultivate.[6] Aside from his short commentary on the *Heart Sūtra*,[7] he does not speak much about Prajñā specifically elsewhere in his writing. Nonetheless, like the young Hui-neng, Prajñā frequently if not continually arose in Dōgen's mind, as we can see throughout the *Shōbō-genzō*. See, for example, his well-known summary of the Way in the *Genjō-kōan*:

To study the Buddha Way is to study the self. To study the self is to forget the self. To forget the self is to be confirmed by the ten-thousand things. To be confirmed by the ten-thousand things is to drop off body and mind and to drop off the body and mind of others. No trace of this realization remains and this no-trace is continued endlessly.[8]

The first two sentences relate to Dhyāna: "To study the Buddha Way is to study the self. To study the self is to forget the self." Then Prajñā enters: "To forget the self is to be confirmed by the ten-thousand things." This is the key. Once confirmed by birdsong or the wind or a word or a blow, Prajñā might arise frequently, but until then the still small voice one hears mentioned so often in religious literature is probably just psychological feedback. Any Zen Buddhist teacher worth her or his salt will not let up until the confirmation is truly intimate.

A monk asked Tung-shan, "Among the Three Bodies of the Buddha, which one does not fall into categories?"
Tung-shan said, "I am always intimate with it."[9]

As I indicated earlier, the Three Bodies of the Buddha are the Dharmakāya, the Sambhogakāya, and the Nirmānakāya: the pure and clear, empty body; the body of blissful harmony; and the body of uniqueness and variety. Tung-shan said, "I am always intimate with it." *It* is the one that does not fall into such categories. Tung-shan is intimate with it and we should understand that intimacy is a synonym for wisdom in the old texts. And what is wisdom? For Bodhidharma, the great founder of Ch'an, and thus Zen Buddhism, it lies in not knowing. He didn't even know who he was and said so to the emperor of China.[10] This is the hard nut of complementarity that nourishes ardent students.

Later, a monk asked Tung-shan's successor Ts'ao-shan

about Tung-shan's response, "I am always intimate with it." Ts'ao-shan said, "If you want my head, cut it off and take it."[11] When you are intimate, you have forgotten yourself. When you are not intimate, you are in your head. "I don't need that," says Ts'ao-shan; cut it off and take it away! And keep taking it away, as Dōgen said. "This no-trace is continued endlessly."

Prajñā is probably best known to students of Zen Buddhism through the *Prajñāpāramitā-hridaya-sūtra*, or *Heart Sūtra*. Although we translate "*hridaya*" as "heart," it actually means "mind essence" in this context. The *Heart Sūtra* is the mind essence of the *Mahāprajñāpāramitā-sūtra*, a treasury of Mahāyāna wisdom in six hundred Chinese fascicles. The *Heart Sūtra* is the treasury of perennial wisdom in just twenty-eight lines. It begins:

> *Avalokiteshvara Bodhisattva, practicing deep Prajñā Pāramitā,*
> *clearly saw that all Five Skandhas are empty, transforming anguish and distress.*
> *Shāriputra, form is no other than emptiness, emptiness no other than form;*
> *form is exactly emptiness, emptiness exactly form;*
> *sensation, perception, formulation, consciousness are also like this.*
> *All things are essentially empty—not born, not destroyed;*
> *not stained, not pure; without loss, without gain.*

The Sūtra goes on, but only to amplify these basic points.

To comment from the beginning: "Avalokiteshvara Bodhisattva, practicing deep Prajñā Pāramitā . . . " Avalokiteshvara is a Bodhisattva in the Indian Buddhist pantheon, whose name means "sovereign observer," a deity of mercy who saves supplicants who call his name. The title Bodhisattva is usually left untranslated, though Thomas Cleary renders it "Enlightening Being." This is close to the etymology, though it should be amplified. The Bodhisattva is one who is becoming enlightened and enlightening others. The vow of the Bodhisattva, to postpone full and complete enlightenment until all beings are enlightened, empowers the world with a liberated life of renunciation.

In China the Bodhisattva Avalokiteshvara became the androgynous Kuan-yin, perhaps more feminine than masculine, with two names that we pronounce "Kanzeon" and "Kanjizai" in Sino-Japanese. Kanzeon, or Kannon for short, is the "one who perceives sounds of the world," one who becomes enlightened by birdsong and the wind—and one who internalizes the innumerable sounds of suffering. Thus she embodies wisdom and love as a single virtue. Her personal process of realization is at the same time the process of world realization. In the *Saddharmapundarīka-sūtra*, the *Lotus Sūtra*, it is clear that Kanzeon responds to supplications like Avalokiteshvara.[12] Her devotional role carries over into Zen Buddhist practice, but she is also our own personal deepest inspiration. She is not separate from my own body or yours and she lives a life of offering.

When you see an illustrated copy of the *Heart Sūtra*, you find a figure that is unmistakably Kanzeon, but the text in Sino-Japanese gives her name as Kanjizai. She is the same personage with a different name, "one who perceives the unfettered self," one who is free and sees the source of freedom.

"Practicing deep Prajñā Pāramitā"—Hakuin Ekaku Zenji has a lot of fun with this line in his *Dokugo Shingyō* ("Poison Words for the Heart"):

Bah! Gouging out healthy flesh and creating open wounds. How strange, this Prajñā of hers. Just what is it like? "Deep"? "Shallow"? Like river water? Can you tell me what kind of Prajñā has deeps and shallows? I'm afraid it's a case of mistaken identity, confusing the pheasant with the phoenix.[13]

How can wisdom be qualified? Pāramitā is "perfection," both the state and the act. Even the action of becoming perfect cannot be deep or shallow. Deep and shallow are relative, comparative terms. What would be the comparison? Hakuin goes on to spoof the entire Sūtra. He makes his point that "words do not convey the fact."[14] But they do convey important hints, so we solemnly intone this Sūtra every day.

"Clearly saw that all Five Skandhas are empty, transforming anguish and distress." The Five Skandhas are the five bundles of perception: forms and colors of the world, sensation, perception, formulation, and consciousness. Reference is to the bare power of things of the world and perceptions of them—the basic functions, so to speak. Formulation, for example, is the mental engine of conception rather than the product that is conceived. Even these functions are without substance or essence, the Sūtra says. The usual human way of concocting an agent for them, of bringing them together as a self-centered entity, gives rise to all kinds of distress through offense, defense, and exploitation.

It is a peak experience, a great relief, to realize that perceptions and things perceived are without substance. The world comes back with all its ego-centered and ego-created pain and anguish, but Kanjizai knows about their causes now and is liberated from their blind compulsions. Emotions rise and fall but the empirical self is not sitting there waiting to strike back. Affinity does not necessarily become lust; betrayal does not necessarily lead to hatred. The one who has defended the self can at last acknowledge that very same self as a particular and peculiar form of the essential mystery. He or she is then freed to save the many beings including the one who saves. The way of practice has opened out at last.

Kanjizai then calls out, "Form is no other than emptiness;

emptiness no other than form." Keizan Jōkin Zenji puts this poetically:

> *Though we find clear waters ranging to the vast blue sky in autumn,*
> *how can it compare with the hazy moon on a spring night?*
> *Most people want to have it pure white,*
> *but sweep as you will, you cannot empty the mind.*[15]

Though in peak experiences the Dharmakāya appears, we find that the true pleasure of being human lies not so much in vast emptiness but in the poignant nature of things—the joy of ambiguity and complementarity—of life in the world of difficulties.

"Most people want to have it pure white." In Far Eastern languages, the word *white* also means "colorless, transparent." Most people want to have it totally pure.

"But sweep as you will, you cannot empty the mind." We are beings of thoughts. What kind of thoughts?

A while back I attended a conference on American Buddhism at Ann Arbor and was privileged to meet the Cambodian monk Maha Ghosananda. He sat there on the podium with the other co-leaders of the conference, sometimes deep in meditation and sometimes looking out over the audience and smiling at us. And then he'd be back in to meditation again. Very wonderful. In and out, back and forth, with very pleasant thoughts, I am sure.

Kanjizai then says to her interlocutor Shāriputra, "Form is exactly emptiness; emptiness exactly form"—and goes through the other bundles that form our nature, sensation, perception, formulation, and consciousness—and continues: "All things are essentially empty—not born, not destroyed; not stained, not pure; without loss, without gain." Here we see the Middle Way of the Buddha Dharma. Conceptual dyads are useful in communication but they become invidious when, for example, truth and falsehood become fixed positions that differ from person to person. Misunderstandings turn into anger, and worse. Thus it is not the forms of the world, it is not our perceptions of the forms, that are obstacles. It is the fact that we take them as ultimate verities. The Sūtra itself is laughable, as Hakuin points out.

QUESTIONS AND RESPONSES

Q. In the *Heart Sūtra* we find the term "anuttara-samyak-sambodhi." Does it translate?

R. Yes, it does. "Peerless, unsurpassed, all pervading enlightenment." Something like that.

Q. Does that translate a little further?

R. It means you really got it. But what have you got? Emptiness? Fullness? David Kalupahana is very clear that *Nirodha* and realization must be distinguished.[16] *Nirodha* is extinction, the experience of complete emptiness. Everything is gone. It is what Dōgen Zenji speaks of as "body and mind dropped away"—the peak experience. On the other hand, realization or Prajñā is the dropped-away body and mind—the practice afterward. Bodhisattvas live by Prajñā Pāramitā when they have seen clearly that there is no eye, ear, nose, tongue, body, mind.

Q. So there is a sequence: extinction and then the life of realization?

R. For some people there is a lapse between. It might be just a few moments, it might be a few days or even weeks of lingering in an empty state—wandering around in a daze. Ultimately, however, you must step off the top of that pole of emptiness. Then, as Ch'ang-sha says, the whole world will be your entire body.[17]

Of course, in the daily life of even the most accomplished student, conditions change. Prajñā arises in the mind—and falls. There is a saying in Japanese monasteries that if you have a deep kenshō, your skin does not stop quivering for three days. But it does stop.

Q. How does this link with our work with *Mu*?

R. That is an important point. I have said that you should be doing *Mu* with an open mind, with open perceptions, so that the sounds of the birds go right through, the sound of the clappers and bells go right through. The point here is that those birds and those clappers and those bells are also expressing *Mu*. *Mu* outside and *Mu* inside become one. This is a beginning stage of extinction, of Nirodha. As Wu-men says, "You are like a mute person who has had a dream."[18]

Q. I remember that you said that the line "Far beyond delusive thinking, right here is Nirvāna" is literally "Far beyond upside-down thinking, right here is Nirvāna."[19]

R. Yes, delusive thinking is really upside down. As Ching-ch'ing said, "Ordinary people are upside down, falling into delusion about themselves and pursuing outside objects."[20] Prajñā is a matter of experiencing the raindrops so intimately that they fall within—and "within" has no bounds. This is Nirvāna. I have to work on that.

Q. One gets the impression that when there is an experience of emptiness, then that's it! There is no suffering or fear after that. I think it can be very useful to look at moment-to-moment Nirvānas. We need to renew ourselves moment by moment, even after having an experience of emptiness. Zen books seem to suggest that the experience of emptiness is a complete transformation. Perhaps for some people it might be, but I suspect for most it's not.

R. You know, the Four Noble Truths are concerned about extinction. It is set forth as the Third Truth, then the Fourth Truth is the way to attain it—the Eightfold Path. So in Classical

Buddhism we get the impression that with the experience of emptiness, that's it! However, both Classical Buddhism and Mahāyāna offer paths afterward. Moreover, both paths have their limitations—Classical Buddhism was directed toward character perfection. The importance of compassion was stressed, but not the fact that the other is no other than myself. In Zen Buddhism, the various kōans stress the unity and the harmony of the world and the self, but there is not much emphasis on character perfection. So both sides have strengths and lacks. We need to somehow bring in more of Classical Buddhism to Zen.

In Classical Buddhism, as it is practiced today in Theravāda centers, character change is stressed from the outset of practice. People are offered all kinds of moral exercises before they are directed toward Nirodha. You're trained to watch your tendency to be angry, greedy, selfish, and so on.

Q. The practice of Vipassanā is to be with the experience of whatever is happening in the body-mind. Essentially it is being with the Five Skandhas. There are the three practices of Shīla, Samādhi, and Prajñā. But they're not step by step; it's all together. It's not like you progress from one to the other. You don't start with morality and go to meditation.

R. I am sure you are right. You have had more practical experience with the discipline of Vipassanā than I have. In any case, I have the sense that somehow in Zen Buddhist practice we must build in more preparation, maybe in conjunction with the early stages of zazen. We should not just toss people into zazen, sink or swim, whatever their condition and frame of mind. One of my teachers assigned *Mu* to everyone right away. I can't follow that path.

Q. Do you mean that we should offer practice in ethical development?

R. If you are not settled ethically, you are not really ready to sit there with a quiet mind.

Q. Aren't the ethics there already?

R. They are there in one form or another, perhaps just in an inchoate form. We talked about that in conjunction with the Second Pāramitā. They evolve to some degree with zazen, since you are learning about your limitations and strengths as you sit there. However, I think that ethics should be set forth as particular handles in spiritual evolution to give it particularity.

Q. Practicing the Brahma-vihāras, the Four Noble Abodes, used to be traditional in Chinese monasteries. Why wasn't that kept as time has gone on?

R. I suppose that Confucian forms gradually supplanted them.

Q. Could they be the foundation block that you're talking about?

R. Yes, or something similar. We don't have the Confucian forms imprinted in our Western psyche. The earlier Indian forms seem more compatible somehow. In any case, it would be good to find some way to work such archetypes into our meditation.

Q. I've experienced the Four Noble Abodes as a meditation in Theravāda practice. In fact, I understood that when students came to a monastery, the Four Abodes took up their first year of practice. Loving-kindness, compassion, unselfish joy, equanimity—you can start anywhere. I usually start with the one that's most difficult, with myself. I show compassion toward myself and then extend it to someone I care about. Then I pick out someone who is kind of neutral and extend compassion toward that person. Then to someone unpleasant. Then to the whole world. I assume that's what you're talking about when you speak of changing character.

R. Chararacter is the formation of one's qualities. It is the tree that grew from the seed that appeared at your birth. The problem is how we habitually use our qualities.

Anne Aitken and I had an interesting experience visiting the Happy Valley School in Ojai, California, for a commencement. It was the thirtieth reunion for one of the classes that we taught there. We were seeing people forty-eight years old whom we hadn't seen since they were eighteen. And younger people, too, because we had taught them also. So some twelve-year-olds were now forty-two. They hadn't changed that much! I could see the same qualities but whereas some had lived fulfilling lives, some had not. Some had ripened, some hadn't. They became young people again, doing the folk dances that they had done when they were young. Galumphing around!

Q. Maybe we could start to talk about character development or maturation or blossoming.

R. Yes, because some people have unreasonable expectations of Zen practice. They feel tired of themselves. "I don't want to be me anymore." Their practice doesn't work because their expectations aren't real. You don't become somebody else.

Q. But sometimes your attitudes about yourself do change.

R. Yes, realizing that this very body is the Buddha can certainly bring an honest kind of self-esteem that might have been missing before.

Q. Could you talk a little bit about the importance of finding and having a teacher?

R. Yes, two important questions—finding and having. There's a book called *Zen without Zen Masters.* I haven't read it. Maybe enough said there. [Laughter] By our nature, we fool ourselves so easily that it is important to have someone we trust to the very bottom to hold up the mirror and say, "This is how you're coming across." Without a true teacher you plateau too soon; the Sangha plateaus too soon. You are left thinking zazen is itself enlightenment, not realizing that you aren't doing zazen. There are depths beyond depths. With a true teacher you can follow the exacting path that leads on and on.

In the old days in China it was said that if you aspire to find a true teacher one will appear. Do you know the story of Chü-chih who was given his comeuppance by the nun True World? He was doing zazen in his lonely hut in the forest. She came in and walked three times around his seat and said, "If you can say an appropriate word I will take off my hat." He couldn't answer. So she walked around his seat three times again and said, "If you can say an appropriate word I will take off my hat." He still couldn't answer. And it happened a third time. She gave up. As she was leaving he called to her and said, "It's getting dark, won't you stay the night?" and she said, "I will stay the night if you can say an appropriate word." He couldn't. So he realized that he couldn't get anywhere by himself and decided, "I will go out into the world and find myself a true teacher." He packed up all his gear and he sat nodding over his pack waiting for the dawn. The tutelary deity of the mountain appeared and said, "Don't go! In three days a true master will come." And sure enough in three days a true master came by.[21]

Well, it's a nice story but it doesn't work for us. In our circumstances there are few true teachers. We can't just wait for one to appear.

Q. How do you know a teacher is genuine?

R. It's partly intuition, I think. I remember Nakagawa Sōen Rōshi's story of how he found his own teacher, Yamamoto Gempō Rōshi. The young Nakagawa was a student at Tokyo University, very enthusiastic about Zen practice. He organized the Tokyo University Zazen-kai, which still meets to this day. One day he went to a neighboring temple to borrow a *kyosaku*, the stick of encouragement. He found that a rōshi was to give a teishō, so he stayed to listen. Afterward he put his hand over his abdomen and said, "I felt something warm here." That's an important test, I think.

We have learned, however, that intuition can't always be trusted. You must check out your prospective teacher. Is this person accessible?—open to criticism?—open to challenge? Do the senior students seem mature? Are they friendly? Is anything hush-hush? Are administrative meetings open to ordinary members? Is there a poetical ring to the teishōs? Do they include humor?

You need to find the place and the teacher where you feel warmest and most comfortable—and also where your basic criteria are met. Then your task is to take the weak points with the strong. I was present when an elderly man met his new grand-daughter-in-law for the first time. He embraced her and said, "Make him a good husband." Make your new teacher a good rōshi.

Q. How about when you have several teachers within the same tradition—not necessarily just one?

R. It depends upon how intimately related they are within that one tradition. For example, in the United States, Fukushima Rōshi and Sasaki Rōshi teach in very different ways even though they are within the same Rinzai tradition. I call to mind the Hindu proverb "You don't strike water by starting new wells." I think that when your circumstances allow it, you should settle with one teacher.

Still, the time might come when you think of changing teachers. Consider the implications carefully before you make your move. One way or another, it will be an important milestone in your practice career—an epoch in the old sense of epoch: a switch, a pivot. Once you take such a step, then follow through without looking back.

Having said that, I should comment about visiting other centers. People come to me and say, "Do you think it's all right if I do a Vipassanā retreat?" I am likely to say—in fact I don't ever remember saying anything else—"Sure, it's okay." Vipassanā practice, Vajrayāna practice, Yoga practice—these will offer useful perspectives. When Zen students are drawn to one or another of them, it usually means that they can profit from the exposure.

Q. What is it to have a relationship with a teacher who comes just occasionally on tour, giving large retreats here and there?

Such a teacher is really more of an inspiration or a hero than a day-to-day guide. You read the books, see the videos, attend a big retreat, but you are following a tradition. Personal contact is lacking, except maybe a ten-minute conversation once or twice a year.

R. It's a different kind of relationship. The constant interaction enjoyed by Nan-ch'üan and Chao-chou for forty years is not possible. At the same time there can be genuine, positive transference. If kōan study is not involved and the local Sangha is viable, then the frequency of encounter might not matter too much. By the fact that it's so occasional those encounters could be very meaningful and inspiring.

Q. Is it possible to have one teacher who focuses on meditation and study, and another who is more devoted to an engaged Buddhism?

R. I think your practice teacher will be the central figure. You can then find inspiration from others who are leading engaged Buddhism, or perhaps from someone who is not a Buddhist—a Catholic Worker, for example, or a Quaker.

Incidentally, you don't have to reach an accord with your teacher on the subject of engaged Buddhism. My teachers were tolerant of my interest in peace and social justice, but they themselves did not take part in any of the actions. In fact, some of them were quite nationalistic during their early days. This didn't shake my faith in them as Zen teachers. Yasutani Rōshi, for example, was a youth in Japan at the time of the Russo-Japanese War, a time when there was more jingoism in that jingoistic country than at any other time in history.

In 1893, Shaku Sōen came to the World Parliament of Religions and gave two talks, one on karma and the other on world peace. Twelve years later he was the head chaplain for the Imperial Navy on his way to Manchuria to encourage the troops to die for their Emperor in their war against Russia. As a teacher of the Dharma, irrespective of culture, he should have gone to live under a bridge. As a Japanese teacher of the

Dharma, he inherited the view handed down from earliest times that the function of Buddhism is to support the Imperial Line. He was not free of his culture, any more than most of us are free of ours—in ways we cannot perhaps see clearly. My attitude would be, "Here is a person who in so many ways is an enlightened teacher, so let's just put this one matter on the shelf and acknowledge that we don't agree about it." Like the rest of us, Shaku Sōen Zenji and Yasutani Rōshi were practicing perfection. Both of them practiced world peace to some degree. If they were still living, probably they would be speaking and acting even more peacefully.

Q. Basically what you're saying here is that one can't change his or her conditioning. People can't change who they are in history and place and how they were raised. I know I've heard you say that being a teacher and engaging in sexual misconduct is improper. But it seems to me that being jingoistic is the same kind of thing.

R. I have to confess that you have a point. Shaku Sōen spoke about karma as well as about world peace at the World Parliament of Religions. He undoubtedly felt that it was his karma to go to Manchuria, and that by following his karma he was being faithful to the Buddha. A Buddhist priest who was drafted and sent to the front lines during World War II explained to me that he had felt the same way. Yet a Zen teacher who was guilty of exploiting the transference of his women students gave me the same kind of justification. "She came to my room in the middle of the night, and I felt it was my karma." Maybe she came to his room, or maybe he went to hers, but the justification is baloney.

There is an important degree of difference here. The jingoistic Zen teacher has a certain belief, however mistaken. On the other hand, the teacher who betrays the transference of his woman student is not acting out of any belief, any conviction, any realization at all. So you don't put that misconduct on the shelf; you recognize it for what it is and take yourself out the door forthwith.

Q. Isn't there a danger that a teacher might have gaps in his or her character that make it hard to see each student clearly?

R. Well, that's what we were talking about earlier. Nan-ch'üan could see that Chao-chou would be a good teacher one day, but did he think that somebody else might also be a good teacher—somebody who didn't pan out? We don't know. The teacher is a human being, inevitably with limited vision, to one degree or another. The student is evolving. Some things that might not show now can appear later.

Q. Does Zen tradition have any safeguards against a teacher's shortcomings?

R. There is a provision for that in the traditional Japanese Rinzai monastery. The senior monks invite the new teacher to serve and they have the power in extremity to dismiss him. It doesn't happen very often at all—but they know they have that power and the rōshi knows they have that power. Those senior monks would not expel their teacher without consulting with priests who have gone out from the temple and are well established in the community. They would invite them in and consult. But ultimately they have the power to say, "Out!"

Q. Can you choose a teacher without choosing a lineage?

R. Pretty hard, I think. All the stuff comes along. However, it would not mean literal acceptance of everything in the lineage. So it gets subtle.

Q. What are the essentials in our lineage?

A. We looked at this in recent Diamond Sangha meetings. We want to become a network rather than a kind of paternal outfit with a center and a bunch of affiliates. So we're asking, "What are we? What do we have in common?" We started out by agreeing: First, we are a lay lineage; second, let's see . . . [Long pause; much laughter] We finally just acknowledged that we have a general agreement about what Dharma is.

My students and my successors really don't feel much connection with the Sanbō Kyōdan, our particular sect in Japan. Only two of the four successors has ever visited there, only one for a weekend of practice. Two of them studied under Yamada Rōshi, but none of them met Yasutani Rōshi. So when we say, "Yes, we belong to the Sanbō Kyōdan lineage," that's something like saying, "I am an American." Well, lots of people are Americans but it means different things to different folks.

SEVEN

COMPASSIONATE MEANS

The Upāya Pāramitā

Upāya literally means "suited to the place or situation." It is skillful means, the way of teaching that fits the persons involved, the time, and the place. Though it is sometimes explained as a way that is strategically correct or relatively expedient, the fundamental meaning is "compassionately appropriate." On the altar of Mahāyāna Buddhist temples, you will find the Buddha Shākyamuni in the center, Mañjushrī, the Bodhisattva of Wisdom on one side, and Samantabhadra, the Bodhisattva of Great Compassionate Action, on the other. Prajñā and Upāya are the two essential qualities of Buddhahood. In the down-to-earth vocabulary of Zen Buddhism, they are the "head" and "tail."

> *A monk asked Chiu feng, "How about when there is a head but no tail?"*
>
> *Chiu-feng said, "After all, that is not sublime."*
>
> *The monk asked, "How about when there is a tail but no head?"*
>
> *Chiu-feng said, "Trying one's utmost but having no power."*[1]

As I keep saying, there is nothing helpful in the wisdom of the one who just sits motionless under the Bodhi tree musing about karma and the transitory nature of life. On the other hand, as I also keep saying, there can only be burnout in the daily stress of helping others if there is no inspiration, as social workers, teachers, and nurses know to their sorrow.

Upāya is also called "garden equipment" in the Zen Buddhist texts. Truly compassionate means are likely to be quite homey and not obviously designed for great realization. Chao-chou was a master of the unobtrusive Upāya:

> *Yen-yang asked Chao-chou, "What if I have nothing with me?"*
>
> *Chao-chou said, "Throw it away."*
>
> *Yen-yang said, "If I have nothing with me, what can I throw away?"*
>
> *Chao-chou said, "In that case, keep holding it."*[2]

If it is really true that there is nothing at all, then surely it is an error to hang onto it. Yen-yang persists, however, and Chao-chou says very gently, perfecting his Upāya, "You're not listening, so for now nothing itself can be your practice." It is said that this gentle nudge brought Yen-yang to understand what nothing really is.

When I was a boy, we had a family joke called Yebut. If my brother or I was criticized by our parents, we would say, "Yeah, but. . . ." Everybody would then chorus, "Yebut! Yebut!" and we would be obliged to shut up and rethink, "Maybe I wasn't right after all." I hear "Yebut" in adult conversation too. That's too bad. It is only when we are open that we mature. "Our friends and family members guide us as we walk the ancient path."[3]

In our communications workshops at the Koko An Zendō, the main training is listening. This is not just the perfection of a social skill. The other is not separate from myself: the other person, the other bird, the other gecko, the other *Mu* that we have posited out there somewhere. To be open to the other is the Buddha's compassion.

Recently I have been visiting L—— P—— at the Halawa

High Security Facility in Honolulu. We meet in a windowless, air-conditioned room with heavy walls but the slamming of steel doors penetrates our zazen. I asked him, "When you are doing zazen, how do you handle the sounds of doors slamming?" He replied, "I remember that there are many doors." Chao-chou would nod his approval.

A monk asked Chao-chou, "What is Chao-chou?"

Chao-chou said, "East gate, west gate, south gate, north gate."[4]

Chao-chou was known by the name of his town, in keeping with the Chinese custom of naming a monk by his locale. This is reminiscent of the way Duke Kahanamoku used to be known as Mr. Honolulu. We were proud of him as an Olympic champion and later as our sheriff. You may be sure that the people of Chao-chou were proud of their Zen master too. In all modesty, he took the metaphor firmly in hand to reveal his own nature and function.

"Dharma gates are countless; I vow to wake to them."[5] Doors and their sounds are Upāya for L—— P——. He is on the path of the Upāya Pāramitā. This is the path that deals with each stone, each plant, each animal, each person, each word, as a teaching. Each thing is a metaphor. Each incident has primal power that can be uncovered by the skilled teacher. Often the teacher will manufacture the Upāya. A few used the same Upāya over and over, as did Chü-chih, who always raised one finger, and Lu-tsu, who always turned around and faced the wall when someone came for instruction. Subsequent teachers mined those Upāya endlessly.

Every day at mealtime, the Master Chin-niu would personally take the rice bucket and do a dance before the door of the monks' hall. Laughing loudly, he would announce, "Little Bodhisattvas, come and eat your rice!"[6]

It is said that Chin-niu himself acted as cook of his monastery, a position usually assigned to one of the most senior monks. In any case, the monks were constantly being treated to his laughing and dancing. Down through the ages, other teachers have asked, "Suppose you were a monk sitting in the hall when Chin-niu went into his act. How would you respond?" Be careful. Chin-niu is teaching here, not merely announcing dinner.

Chin-niu was a disciple of Ma-tsu. We don't have his dates but he probably held forth in the latter part of the eighth century or the early part of the ninth. A hundred years or so later, his Upāya was still very much alive in the minds of earnest students:

A monk asked Ch'ang-ch'ing, "When the man of old said, 'Little Bodhisattvas, come and eat your rice,' what was his meaning?"

Ch'ang-ch'ing said, "That was a joyful kind of grace before the meal."[7]

The question for the monk and his successors down to our own time then becomes, "How do you see Ch'ang-ch'ing here?" The Upāya is thus enlarged and enriched. And there is more. The bamboo telegraph conveyed Ch'ang-ch'ing's response to other monasteries of the time:

A monk asked Ta-kuang, "Ch'ang-ch'ing says, 'A joyful grace before the meal.' What is his meaning?"

Ta-kuang did a dance. The monk bowed. Ta-kuang asked, "What have you seen that you make a bow?" The monk did a dance.

Ta-kuang said, "You fox bogey!"[8]

Ta-kuang obviously felt that the monk was caught up in the original Upāya, unable to be himself. So the question is, "You are challenged by Ta-kuang to express your realization of Ch'ang-ch'ing's meaning, how do you respond? What is your joyous grace?"

And there is still more. Hsüeh-tou, compiler of *The Blue Cliff Record*, comments two generations later about Chin-niu's rollicking conduct before the hall, "Although he acted in such a way, he was not being cordial."[9] The question for us then becomes, "What is Hsüeh-tou's point here?" The primal power of Chin-niu's dance still has not been used up.

Notice that students themselves continued the Upāya by asking about it. Yasutani Rōshi said, "You should always ask." Here is a case where a monk thought he had it and when he found he didn't, he demanded to know where he had gone wrong:

Ma-ku came to Chang-ching. Carrying his bell staff, he circled Chang-ching's seat three times, brought his staff to the floor, shaking the bells, and stood straight.

Chang-ching said, "Right, right."

Ma-ku came to Nan-ch'üan, circled his seat three times, brought his staff to the floor, shaking the bells, and stood straight.

Nan-ch'üan said, "Not right, not right."

Ma-ku said, "Chang-ching said, 'Right, right,' and Your Reverence says, 'Not right, not right.' Why is that?"

Nan-ch'üan said, "Chang-ching is right, but you are not right. Your action is the movement of the wind. Finally it will perish."[10]

Circumambulation is a perennial ritual that has a role in Zen Buddhist ceremony as it does in the ceremonies of most religions from the primal to the contemporary. Standing straight, bringing one's staff firmly to the floor, shaking the bells in the process—surely this is a valid presentation, the Tathāgata himself coming forth from nowhere into the world.

"Right, right." Chang-ching approves, but with dialogues of monks continuing from teacher to teacher in the process of pilgrimage in those days, he probably knew that he was only the first player in the case. Nan-ch'üan watched the same mime and took the occasion to show Ma-ku how his action was not at all like a firmly rooted tree but like the wind itself, blowing first from one direction, then from another, and finally dying away. It is right to sit motionless in the hall, right to walk firmly to see the teacher, right to stand forth with dignity. But as we say in Hawai'i, "All form but no shape." With compassionate Upāya Nan-ch'üan hints to Ma-ku that there might be a dimension he has not yet entered.

Perhaps Ma-ku was feeling a little defensive when he asked, "Chang-ching said, 'Right, right,' but Your Reverence said, 'Not right, not right.' Why is that?" We can assume, however, that he was also opening himself for Nan-ch'üan's words.

This *I*, and each *I*, is a center for the Upāya—not the ego-centered *I*, but the Bodhisattva *I*. All Upāyas are directed to the Bodhisattva, so it is important to take them to heart in that dimension. Zen Buddhist practice is set up as Upāya: our zazen, our dōjō schedule, our leadership, the mealtime ritual, and all the rest of it. And as L—— P—— teaches us, there are Upāyas everywhere. The rooster crowing in the early morning is an Upāya. The sound of a stone striking a stalk of bamboo was an Upāya for Hsiang-yen. Let's look at kōans as Upāya for a moment.

My first teacher, Senzaki Sensei, had a tea bowl with a spiral design on the inside. He would hold up this bowl and say, "Does this spiral go around to the right from the top or to the left from the bottom?" None of us could answer. A long time later I read an account of an American professor of philosophy who visited a Zen teacher in Japan. He asked the teacher, "What is a kōan?" The teacher said, "Well, when the water goes down the spout, does it go around to the right or to the left?"

The philosopher said, "I don't know." So according to this account, the Zen teacher twirled his finger in the air. When I read that, I suddenly understood Senzaki Sensei's meaning and I knew that he would not approve of just twirling a finger.

Can you show a better response? When I read a draft of this chapter to members of the Koko An Zendō, I stood up at this point and twirled myself around. That's taking it to heart, I should think. The problem with most of us is that we don't let ourselves be involved. We hide and don't allow ourselves to be touched. This deeply ingrained tendency is directly addressed in kōan work. Here, for example, is Yün-men in Case 6 of *The Blue Cliff Record*:

> *Yün-men addressed his assembly and said, "I do not ask you about before the 15th of the month. Come, give a phrase about after the 15th."*
>
> *Nobody could say anything so he answered instead, "Every day is a good day."*[11]

The fifteenth of the month is the day of the full moon on the lunar calendar and by analogy it is the day of full realization. "How about after realization?"—Yün-men is asking, what about you in your daily affairs after you have shared the Buddha's experience under the Bodhi tree?

Nobody could answer. Nobody understood the hook: Before or after realization, one's nature is essentially the same. Yün-men is urging everyone to acknowledge their home in that fundamental, expansive place. In his response to his own question, he seems to be saying that everything happens for the best in this best of all possible worlds. But even a Zen Buddhist teacher's life is up and down, zig and zag. Sometimes I feel as though it is mostly down and zag. It is important to be open to Yün-men's prescription for our uneasy hearts.

The checking question for this case would be something like, "Do you mean to tell me that the day you run over a child with your car is a good day?" Involve yourself here. Dharma gates open constantly, but upon what do they open?

QUESTIONS AND RESPONSES

Q. I would like to ask a question about Upāya. How can the organized system of traditional kōan practice be used as a teaching that would be appropriate for individual persons?

R. I am always gratified when a student comes to me and says, "You know, the kōan we worked through last time just fit my present situation." This is what Jung called synchronicity. My sense is that synchronicity is not a kind of divine coincidence, but the outcome of touching the perennial, where everything is in sync. When you really hit bottom with a kōan, then it will cast light on whatever is happening in your daily life.

You can generally trust the system because the kōans we use are those that have proved over the centuries to be especially efficacious. When they don't seem so meaningful, part of the reason might be a lack of affinity. But another part of the reason might be that you are just not ready.

It seems that in the time just before, during, and just after the T'ang period, when there was a great efflorescence of Zen, some especially talented people could come to full and complete understanding with just a couple of Dharma encounters. For example, the author of *Cheng-tao ke*, Yung-chia, is known as the "Master Who Spent One Night with the Ancestor"—with Hui-neng, that is. He was called that because that's what happened. He just came one afternoon and had his realization. Yes, more than realization, his deep understanding—then he started to leave. Hui-neng said, "Why don't you spend the night?" He spent the night, but that was his only contact. In such an inspiring culture, a random way of teaching emerged—or maybe not random so much as a way of teaching that was not systematized. But everything is in flux and everything flows. That period of illumination faded and we have kept the spark alive through a certain systematizing.

I'll give you another example, this one about Fu Ta-shih, whose kōan "With hands of emptiness, I take hold of the plow" we take up early in the practice. He is venerated for his great understanding within the Zen school, but he had nothing to do with Zen. He lived at the same time as Bodhidharma, but apparently they never met. Yet we include his kōans right there with the others. He appeared at this time of great flowering of Zen understanding where a bit later Ma-tsu could have eighty-two Dharma successors.

Speaking of not being ready for certain kōans, there are a few that took me a long time to resolve even partially. For example, I have started to make sense only recently of Chao-chou's "Throwing the ball on the swift current":

> *A monk asked Chao-chou, "Has the newborn baby the sixth sense or not?" Chao-chou said, "Throwing the ball on the swift current." The monk wasn't happy with that so he went to T'ou-tzu and asked, "What does 'throwing the ball on the swift current' mean?" And T'ou-tzu said, "Moment by moment it never stops flowing."*[12]

When I did that kōan with Yamada Rōshi, I got some sense of it, but not much. I couldn't understand Yuan-wu's commentary on the case very well either. So that's why I suggest that you keep notes. Rereading them, you will find great valleys and mountains in a landscape that seemed flat before.

Q. Do you think William James ever read that kōan?

R. No, but I see your point. William James was the first to use the term "stream of consciousness." He had some familiarity with Buddhism and wrote a bit about it, but the affinity of

James and Buddhism is not a matter of historical connection or influence.

Q. What about those teachers who water down the essence in the name of Upāya?

R. Yes, it is possible to water it down and it is possible to show everything and still not communicate successfully. Some teachers, if you can call them teachers, water things down so much that the real point is lost. Take, for example, the book *The Sound of One Hand.* It's the so-called kōan answer book. Tom Cleary's recent *No Barrier* is philosophically much better than *The Sound of One Hand,* but it also waters experiences down. I challenge anyone to read either of those books and then come to dokusan and make your presentation on the basis of what you have read. You won't last beyond a single checking question. Kōan study is not a matter of opening an esoteric door or unlocking a puzzle. It is a matter of realizing what you already know.

At the same time, there is a good deal in Zen practice that should be demystified. Much too much is just left to the student to reinvent. One of Harada Rōshi's great contributions to the practice was his orientation talks. He laid everything out that could be laid out. I don't think we could, any of us, be here if he had not decided to break precedent in such a way.

Q. What sort of thing would he give in an orientation talk?

R. First of all, he would go into zazen in detail: how to sit, how to hold your head, how to lower your eyes, where to put your hands, how to count your breaths, how to do breath counting—exhalation only, inhalation only, exhalation and inhalation—how to do shikantaza. He would take up the various kinds of distractions and delusions that one can fall into. Then he would talk about the so-called different kinds of Zen, which we translate as attitudes in Zen practice. He would talk about what the dokusan procedure is: why we recite sūtras, what Sōtō practice is, what Rinzai practice is, and, in his own case, what his own practice was. *Taking the Path of Zen* is based on Harada

Rōshi's orientation talks, as they have been modified by Yasutani Rōshi and Yamada Rōshi.

Q. Can you talk about the misuse of Upāya?

R. By definition, there cannot be misuse of Upāya. Distinguish between Upāya and unresolved stuff that is simply projected on others.

Q. A teacher I respect was asked, "How are we to understand actions of a teacher that do not seem skillful?" He answered, "Every act of the teacher is an act of Upāya." That is very much the way of some Buddhist masters. A teacher is never to be questioned. Every act, whatever it is, is to be taken as skillful means. I think of that often. I didn't say anything at that time, but now I think it sums up one of the worst dangers that is evident in some of the Buddhist communities.

R. Yes. I would be scared to be in a position where everything I did was seen as the action of an enlightened Bodhisattva. Phew! That only leads to trouble. The Tibetans understand this very well. The Sixth Dalai Lama disregarded his vows quite openly and his senior lamas acknowledged that he was not on the Path of Enlightenment.[13]

Q. What does Yamada Rōshi say about Upāya?

R. "The purpose of Zen practice is the perfection of character." I understand him to mean this: As we realize "interbeing," to use Thich Nhat Hanh's term, we perfect our character. Body and mind drop away in the experience of extinction, Nirodha. With this experience of completely forgetting the self, we find that we are not separate from others. With the peak experience of forgetting the self informing us, we act in accordance with the needs of our circumstances, the needs of others and, of course, our own needs. We have to feed ourselves and sustain ourselves, find ways to allow ourselves to grow and mature further. In this long, gradual process, we become more and more sensitive to the Upāyas that constantly appear.

Q. This sounds a bit abstract or metaphysical.

R. Oh, it has nothing to do with metaphysics. Perhaps Yamada Rōshi used metaphysical terminology. Or I am using it. But we are trying to say that with this experience we learn better how to take things to heart—and how to act accordingly.

Q. Rōshi, you said this Pāramitā is a call for being alert or for being open.

R. The Pāramitās as expressions of perfection show the way of conduct. Probably I should adjust the emphasis here to the cultivation of compassion in oneself. Chao-chou is maybe the greatest example. So gentle and so full of love, really. Remember Case 52 in *The Blue Cliff Record:*

> *A monk asked Chao-chou, "I have long heard about the great bridge of Chao-chou, but I have come and found only a simple log bridge."*
>
> *Chao-chou said, "You don't see the stone bridge. You only see the simple log bridge."*[14]

The bridge just outside the city of Chao-chou was a famous landmark—it's still there, a great archaeological wonder, constructed in the seventh century. People came, and still come from far and wide to see it. Of course there is a pun here. Chao-chou, named for his place, is one who allows you to cross over.

Well, the conversation goes on from there with its kōan points, but see how generous Chao-chou is. "Oh, is that so? You only see a simple log bridge. You don't see the famous stone bridge. Is that so?" Or how about his encounter with Yen-yang, "Oh, you can't throw 'nothing' away? In that case, please keep carrying it." How his monks must have been struck by Chao-chou's gentle compassion, just the barest nudge along the way! So Upāyas require that you be open to the other.

Q. Are there limitations to this openness to the other that have to be recognized?

R. I'm not sure. When you are completely open to the other, you can see the weaknesses and neuroses, can't you? When I first started going to the Waiawa Prison, one of the inmates who was working with me was very critical of the drug program there. Then I met the director of that program and he invited me to visit. It happened to be the weekend of Thanksgiving. They had a party, so I was invited and had a meal with everybody. I was very impressed by that drug program, by the genuine attitudes of all the inmates and the staff. Actually I couldn't tell the staff from the inmates, except that some of the staff were women.

So the next time we had our little zazen-kai at Waiawa, I remarked, "What a great program that seems to be! Boy, if I were in here, I would want to be involved, just to be in that atmosphere." Silence. The next thing I know, my friend was applying to get into the program. I don't think I was as neat in my expression as Chao-chou might have been in those circumstances, but I think that for once I was gentle in making a suggestion. The program was full, so it will be a while before my friend can get into it, but he did change. He was able to acknowledge, at least to himself, that he was resisting for reasons that weren't particularly admirable.

Q. But not all our Ancestors were so gentle. We read about students who come to see the teacher and get kicked in the butt. Our tradition includes violent kinds of skillful means. They appear to have been appropriate sometimes.

R. Yes, there are a few such cases, well, quite a few, especially cases of using the stick. But such cases as Ch'ang sha wrestling Yang-shan to the ground and stomping on him are not usual.[15] They appear, but they're not usual. But you're right. Sometimes rough action can be appropriate means, skillful means. See, Samantabhadra's holding a sword there on the altar, cutting off your delusions and preoccupations. Still, what is rough for us would be mild for some of our Ancestors.

Q. It seems like it's up to the student to determine whether the teacher's means are skillful. Giving oneself up completely smacks of guru worship, and I don't know where to find the middle line.

R. The middle line is your decision: This is the teacher I feel I can trust. I like him and I like the senior students. I have examined the kitchen, so to speak, and know what is being cooked. I resolve to eat this food. In a very real sense, you are giving yourself up. It is a calculated risk, but so is a new marriage or a new career. Once you plunge in, you devote yourself to making things work. Particularly at the beginning, you will have to accept instructions and situations that run contrary to your previous ways. Eat all the food with your trust that it is good for you.

Speaking of food, once at the old Maui Zendō one of our community members stayed for lunch. I knew he was a vegan. While we were standing around the table in preparation for the mealtime service, he picked up his bowl of soup and sniffed it. I gave him hell for that right on the spot. I said, "You know very well that we serve only vegetables, fruit, and grains here. Your act of picking up the bowl like that is very rude and shows lack of trust."

If the food is edible, then please eat everything. I am not a guru, but at the same time, you really can't get into the practice if you hold a reserved attitude and smell everything suspiciously. This attitude will limit every part of your practice.

Q. Rōshi, isn't that sort of reservation appropriate as a way to avoid the abuse of students by teachers?

R. Of course you should be careful and not invest until you are reasonably confident. Even after that, if the food makes you sick, you leave. You don't lose your self-reliance just because you have developed special affection or gratitude.

Q. That doesn't give a very clear signal to someone who might extend his or her trust to the wrong teacher. At some point a person has to make a break.

R. They certainly do and it can be painful. Nothing is more conducive to psychological collapse or breakdown. I first encountered a wrong teacher right here in this zendō, when within a few weeks of each other two women had nervous breakdowns. I couldn't understand it, and to make a long story short, I found out on working with people in the mental health field that a monk who was living here had become involved with both women. Some people remark about such cases that the women bear some of the responsibility because they are too trusting and too naive. I can't see it that way. If a naive person comes here, I want to respect that naiveté and not shake it.

Q. Rōshi, when you speak about transference as a necessary process, I take it you're using that term in the standard psychological way, where people would approach the teacher as they would a therapist, in a very sort of open, childlike way, and maybe project a parent onto the teacher.

R. Yes, and it can be very difficult for the teacher. I find that I'm wearing Daddy's face and I don't know who Daddy is. It's more difficult for me than for a therapist because the therapist gradually gains some idea about Daddy. But just as the therapist seeks to put the student firmly on her or his own feet, so I seek to do the same.

I have to this day a very special feeling for the therapist that I worked with thirty-five years ago, just as one has a special feeling for one's parents after one is adult. That special feeling continues, I think, but the self-reliance builds and, I hope very soon, people are able to argue back, and say, "I don't agree with you about . . . "—and I'm pleased to listen.

Q. Well, so you are saying that transference arises from both sides.

R. Of course. But if the teacher doesn't have the wisdom to cope and to handle that transference appropriately, it's no good. When I said the other day that I couldn't understand exploitive actions, that was not a full picture of my attitude and experience. I was a teacher, or at least a senior student, during the 1960s and there were plenty of occasions where I was in very intimate situations with women students. A couple of times I was a bit like Gandhi, who deliberately tested himself. I never lost it, but I know the temptations. I didn't understand how a teacher who is wonderful in so many respects could give way to them. Now I think I can see more clearly how wisdom and compassion can be relatively profound and yet deeply flawed.

Q. So we really can't expect infallibility on the part of the teacher? I can't really see that we can; I understand there have been gross transgressions.

R. Well, I suppose we shouldn't expect an absolute perfection, but as you say, some transgressions really have been gross. On the other hand, sometimes sexual relations between teachers and students have worked out fine. In the course of my conversations with Brother David, I mentioned the marriages that I know of between pastors and members of their congregations. Catholic priests have disrobed and married former nuns. Somehow they are able to step out of their teacher-student or pastor-disciple roles and do it. The marriages seem to be as happy as any other, or happier.

Q. I guess I was not thinking on a gross level—just that you can't expect everyone to be infallible. I used to have the feeling that if a guy slips it probably means he's fallen apart completely. I keep thinking, "Here's a guy who's repressed himself to get to where he is and suddenly he cracks up!" Like an egg.

R. I'll grant you that possibility.

Q. I just wanted to say after having opened that can of worms, that really wasn't the can I intended to open. [Laughter] I wasn't thinking of teachers taking advantage of students so much as: How can a good teacher help the student stand on his or her own feet? How does that help the student to maintain integrity? Standing on my own two feet, I may feel sure a certain way works for me. How do I face a teacher who says, "Do everything my way"?

R. You have to do this by instinct. Do you feel encouraged? Do you feel put down? This is really the clue. There is a package here. How's the package for you? That's the question you should ask. You can't select bits of the package. The package is the whole thing.

Q. Rōshi, to get back to your food analogy, you suggested that we take everything in, but as time goes on you don't assimilate all of it. How does this work?

R. Oh, you don't keep all of it from day one. For example, I tell people to keep their eyes one-third open. And from day one, people are telling me, "I can't keep my eyes one-third open—I have to close them." Okay, close them.

Q. Well, I'm trying to clarify, there's a fine line here . . .

R. Metaphors can be unclear and self-limiting. Regarding the metaphor of eating, as clearly as I can express it: you get the most out of your practice by assimilating as much as you can. You pass off what you can't handle. You invest, and investment is like anything else: It builds. There are some people who invest from the beginning. Some people come and want to begin formal study with me before we have even met. Some people take a year before they begin dokusan. Look back at Kubota Rōshi's story in *The Three Pillars of Zen*—"Mr. A. K., Insurance Adjuster."[16] He went to see Yasutani Rōshi when he was only seventeen about his feelings of despair after his brother died in a drowning accident. The Rōshi invited him to sit and he joined the Sangha. He had his kenshō three years after he graduated from college during a sesshin with Yasutani Rōshi that Anne and I attended. At the tea after sesshin, he remarked, "For eight years I was not able to follow the Rōshi's instructions." Ānanda was not able to follow the Buddha's instructions for the duration of the Buddha's life. He had to wait and work under Mahākāshyapa. Practice builds.

EIGHT

ASPIRATION

The Pranidhāna Pāramitā

The Pranidhāna Pāramitā is the perfection of Bodhichitta which is, as I have indicated, the aspiration for personal and universal realization and liberation. Bodhichitta is literally "the thought of Bodhi (wisdom)" and at the outset it may simply be the perception that life is short and that people, animals, and plants are having a hard time. Dōgen Kigen writes:

> *The thought of enlightenment has many names, but they all refer to one and the same mind. Ancestor Nāgārjuna said, "The mind that fully sees into the uncertain world of birth and death is called the thought of enlightenment." Thus if we maintain this mind, this mind can become the thought of enlightenment.*[1]

Here the translator, Kazuaki Tanahashi, renders Bodhichitta literally. "Enlightenment" is an accurate translation for Bodhi and is an appropriately paramount word in this context. But be careful not to use it indiscriminately. It is a word, like *love*, that does not belong on postage stamps. Often *realization* is the appropriate term, making real and manifest the vacancy, the harmony, and the uniqueness of all beings and their interdependence.

The Buddha's own Bodhichitta first arose when as a noble

youth he noticed from the elevation of his carriage that there is sickness, old age, and death in this world—and also that some people become monks. Of course it is possible for someone to notice sickness, old age, death, and the presence of religious people without any particular reaction, or with resistance and denial. In such a case, the Way of the Buddha and the other religious paths do not seem to be practical options, at least at the time. Maybe in another year the misery of the world will sink in. The Pranidhāna Pāramitā may then start to make sense, like words on shop signs for the young child.

When it does make sense, one wishes that something could be done about it. Pranidhāna is the formulation of that wish. Probably the earliest Buddhist texts were such formulations, retained today in Theravāda Buddhism in their invocations, for example, "May all beings be free from the notion of property, even with regard to their own bodies! May they be firmly established in Righteousness until they attain the final Liberation! May they not even know the name of Evil!"[2]

Formulations within the Mahāyāna tradition are more likely to express personal involvement. They tend to express responsibility for the welfare of others and often draw inspiration from archetypal personages. The vows of fabled Bodhisattvas to postpone their own complete liberation until all beings are liberated enable them to save those who call out their names. Prominent among these remarkable archetypes is Dharmākara, who became the Buddha Amitābha. In forty-eight vows he refused complete Buddhahood for himself until universal enlightenment could be realized. This empowered his very name, so he promised rebirth in the Pure Land to those who call out *Namu Amida Butsu*, or the equivalent in their own languages, "Veneration to the Buddha Amitābha!"[3]

Another liberating figure is Kshitigarbha (Japanese: "Jizō") the "Earth Treasury Bodhisattva," who has the Earth's power of life. He is the patron of those in terrible misery. "If hells are not empty," he vowed, "I will not become a Buddha."[4] In Japan, Jizō is the patron of fishermen, travelers, and children, especially those children who have died. *Namu Jizō Bosatsu*,

"Veneration to Kshitigarbha Bodhisattva!" You will find his stone image at crossroads shrines throughout the countryside.

Then there is Bhaishajya-guru-Buddha, the Medicine-King Bodhisattva, who is also considered a Buddha. He expressed the total sincerity of his vows by immolating himself. He partook of many kinds of incense, drank the essential oils of various kinds of flowers, and let all this settle for twelve hundred years. Then in the presence of the Buddha "Sun-Moon Brilliance" he wrapped himself in a celestial garment, bathed in perfumed oil, and by his transcendent vow set himself alight. He burned with a brightness that illuminated an incomprehensible number of worlds for another twelve hundred years. All the Buddhas of those worlds simultaneously extolled him, saying, "Good, good, good! This is true zeal. It is called the true-law homage to the Tathāgata."[5] The Medicine-King Bodhisattva was a noble model for the Vietnamese monks who serenely immolated themselves for peace during the civil war in their country.

When one of my friends first looked into the possibility of Buddhist study, she opened D. T. Suzuki's *Manual of Zen Buddhism* to the passage in the long sūtra devoted to Kanzeon where the World Honored One promises that if you are pushed off the highest peak and invoke the name of Kanzeon Bosatsu (Bodhisattva), you will be suspended in the air like the sun.[6] "What *am* I getting into?" she wondered.

What indeed? What is the practical Pranidhāna? These brilliant, ultimate kinds of vows and promises lend deep encouragement to one's personal vows and fuel their efficacy. It takes a while to understand this. How, for example, can one fulfill the Great Vows for All?

The many beings are numberless, I vow to save them;
greed, hatred, and ignorance rise endlessly, I vow to abandon them;
Dharma gates are countless, I vow to wake to them;
Buddha's way is unsurpassed, I vow to embody it fully.[7]

We recite these vows every day, as do most Mahāyāna Buddhists in their services in one form or another and in one translation or another—as our Ancestors recited them down through the years since they were composed in the very earliest Buddhist times. Isshū Miura and Ruth Sasaki comment in *Zen Dust*:

> *For the Mahayana Buddhist, with the true awakening of the desire for enlightenment spontaneously arises the awakening of "the compassionate heart," that is, the desire to share this enlightenment with others.*[8]

But people ask me, "How can I save the many beings?" I respond, "Carry that question with you." It is your daily life kōan and mine, governing all words and deeds—from the inside, as it were. Somewhere I read about a Christian missionary who was retiring after a laudable career in Japan. Someone asked him, "How many people did you convert?" With a broad smile he answered, "Not one." Yet it seems that he held the spirit of conversion and with his labor the whole world was converted.

"Greed, hatred, and ignorance rise endlessly . . . " These are the Three Poisons. They arose endlessly in the minds of our Ancestors in the Dharma—they arise endlessly in our minds and in the minds of everyone everywhere. Join the club. Even Bodhidharma had to deal with them as he sat for those nine years facing the wall at the very end of his life. They are our self-centered thoughts: "how I am; how I was; how I will be." We motivate ourselves with our vows to move from the singular to the plural, to abandon indulgence in the sole self and divert energy to the community. Zazen is the ground for this transformation; daily life is its garden. We practice it together.

"Dharma gates are countless, I vow to wake to them." There is a lot of misunderstanding about this line, even among Japanese Zen Buddhist teachers. I have heard more than one assure students that *gates* is just a tag word with no particular significance. The point is, they say, that you must understand the Dharma in all its ramifications. I feel sure that this is an incomplete explanation. You must wake to the Dharma teaching of the mynahs as they squabble on the lawn, to the wind in the casuarina trees. Who is hearing that sound?

"Buddha's way is unsurpassed, I vow to embody it fully." The parent embodies the role of parent as intimately and personally as possible or the child cannot mature. Outside the home, the machinist embodies the role of machinist as personally as possible—the nurse, the surveyor, the pedestrian, the patient in the doctor's office embody their roles as personally as possible or their function is inadequate and the fabric of society is weakened. Yet the parent can never fully embody the role of parent and is constantly practicing the task of integrating person and parent more and more intimately. The machinist, the nurse, the surveyor, the pedestrian, the patient in the doctor's office too are practicing. In the same way, the Buddhist too is practicing the noble task of embodying the Buddha Way. By practicing the Buddha Way we fulfill it. And we continue to fulfill it endlessly.

In the *Hua-yen ching*, the *Avatamsaka Sūtra*, we read:

> *Bodhisattva Chief-in-Knowledge asked the Bodhisattva Mañjushrī, "How can Bodhisattvas attain faultless physical, verbal, and mental action? How can they attain harmless physical, verbal, and mental action? How can they attain blameless physical, verbal, and mental action . . . ? How can they fulfill kindness, compassion, joy, and equanimity?"*[9]

And so on for two full pages. Mañjushrī replies with a chapter of vows in gāthā form, four-line poems that students have memorized through the ages to help them in the exigencies of daily life. Thomas Cleary, in his comprehensive translation of the *Hua-yen,* uses the third person in rendering those traditional gāthā-vows.

While with their spouses and children
They should wish that all beings
Be impartial toward everyone
And forever give up attachment.[10]

"They" are Bodhisattvas, but really *we* are Bodhisattvas—you and I, developing impartiality and nonattachment as best we can. The use of "they" takes the vow away from us and gives it to hypothetical people far away and long ago. Rather than presuming to rewrite this translation, I offer my own gāthā about family to illustrate the importance of expressing vows personally:

When dissension comes up in the family
I vow with all beings
to suggest we get on with our loving—
who knows if we'll be here next week?[11]

The second line in each of the *Hua-yen* vows is the same, the Bodhisattva practice of turning the Dharma Wheel with everyone and everything. One accepts this practice. Accepting is the first step of practice. The child practices tying her shoelaces. She won't let you show her more than once. She won't let you do it for her. She does it herself, over and over, until she gets it right. The attorney practices law, the physician practices medicine. The vow is the promise to take on the task oneself. Earnest students in ancient days memorized the many vows in the Pure Conduct chapter of the *Hua-yen* to remind (re-mind) themselves through their days to take responsibility for the noble Buddha Way in this circumstance, that circumstance.[12] Write your own vows.

Thus intimate response is the Tao. Kuan-yin is enlightened by the sounds and the forms of the world. Why? Because she allows herself to be intimate. Completely open, she finds her intimacy confirmed. Finding intimacy with all beings, confirming her interbeing with them, she suffers with others. This is com-passion. The Great Vows for All are the vows of Kuan-yin. In taking them, holding them, and acting upon them you fulfill the Pranidhāna Pāramitā.

Checking Buddhist references, I find a number of interesting compounds with Pranidhāna, for example, the "Vow-wheel." With this wheel, you vow and fulfill your vows with all beings. "Vow-food" is another compound, the way of using experiences to confirm and sustain your vows. "Vow-power," "Vow-wisdom," "Vow-conduct," and other compounds are worthy of study.

Taking vows is like learning zazen or learning anything. At first, repeating the Great Vows for All seems awkward and unreal. There doesn't seem to be much connection with daily life. Making one's own vows likewise seems artificial, perhaps excessively moralistic. But soon enough they become integrated and rise spontaneously to mind as our guides, like "Praise God" in the minds of our great-grandparents, like *Hare Ram* in the mind of Gandhi, or like lamenting in the minds of traditional peoples.

Black Elk and his Oglala Sioux compatriots "cried for visions." They went to the mountains to "lament." After listing various purposes for this ancient practice, Joseph Epes Brown remarks, "Perhaps the most important reason for 'lamenting' is that it helps us realize our oneness with all things, to know that all things are our relatives."[13]

"Crying for visions," "lamenting"—these expressions present the passion of perennial aspiration on all religious paths. But there are also aspirations that come and go because they are rooted in self-centered concerns. "When the blood burns, how prodigal the soul/Lends the tongue vows," remarks Polonius in his portentous way.[14] They are words of wisdom nonetheless. Polonius was cautioning Ophelia that the fire of such vows can give more light than heat. "Better it is that thou shouldest not vow, than thou shouldest vow and not pay."[15] It all comes down, as Dōgen reminds us, to will and aspiration.

So the superego sticks in her oar: "Am I really sincere in my passionate desire for Buddhahood? How can I fulfill such lofty vows? Maybe it is better not to make them." This is the perfectionist fallback position again. Yet fulfillment is not anything absolute. It is realized again and again with the vow itself, as Blake realized his in "Milton":

I will not cease from Mental Fight
Nor shall the Sword sleep in my hand
Till we have built Jerusalem
In England's green and pleasant Land.

QUESTIONS AND RESPONSES

Q. Could you say something more about using experiences to sustain our vows?

R. Vows and experience interplay. Your vows direct you to the deepest experience of the real world—the world of interbeing. So do bells, clappers, birdsong, and even the helicopter rattling overhead. So do mountains and clouds and poinciana trees. So does the whiff of incense or the touch of your clothing to your skin when the wind blows. These experiences can reveal interbeing directly, or they can remind you of your vows—and your vows in turn can help you to be open to experience.

We should also be open to the world of human interaction. Dōgen says: "One phrase offered by a loyal servant can have the power to alter the course of the nation. One word given by a Buddha Ancestor cannot fail to turn people's minds."[16] If the governor does not listen to appropriate advice, he or she cannot govern with virtue. It is important to be open to suggestions, to be open to comments, to be open to little hints. "Our friends and family members guide us as we walk the ancient path." This guidance is often very subtle. Usually people don't say, "What a narcissistic person you are!" They will try to frame their guidance more gently and if you aren't listening closely with a forgotten self, you will miss it.

Q. Just today I was talking with a friend from Japan. She said that if someone tromps on your foot in her country, you would say something like, "Oh, I'm very sorry, excuse me, but. . . ." It seems to me that this isn't merely Japanese. In our own culture women are taught to respond like this. Maybe women need to be told something different—that sometimes it is important to speak up very forcefully.

R. Yes, as Dōgen says in the same paragraph from which I quoted just now, "One who does not step forward cannot accept the Buddha's teaching." The Buddha Way is always the Middle Way. Stepping forward, stepping back. What do the circumstances require? Certainly the consistently humble person is often quite neurotic, probably secretly angry. That anger has to come out willy-nilly.

Q. I know that you make decisions all the time in responding to individuals before you. I'm wondering if you make a certain response to women and a certain response to men?

R. No, I don't have set responses. I respond as best I can to the individual man or woman sitting before me. I have assimilated a certain understanding of gender differences over the years, a certain understanding of practice problems, a certain understanding of the Dharma, and of course a personal understanding of particular students as I get to know them. My responses probably arise from a synthesis of all this in relation to the immediate circumstances—of course framed by my own personality. But saying all this still seems to imply that I act from outside. Really, the best teaching is from inside, inside the other, inside the situation.

Q. When we work toward an ideal, such as fulfilling our vows, we work toward it from different directions, so our paths can sometimes be very different. At times it's necessary for one person to do just the reverse of what another would do.

R. Yes, that's what I referred to by action framed by personality. Also, we need to be careful about precedents. I think that we must be conscious that the old teachers were directing themselves exclusively toward ordained men.

Q. That suggests that our teachings might be totally different if we were inheriting a tradition of talks to laywomen.

R. It would be different for sure. Still, I find Dōgen Zenji quite feminine in many ways. For example, in the paragraph I have been quoting there is just one sentence about stepping forward and a total of five sentences about being flexible.

Q. It does get to the point where it's hard to generalize. I think that in Zen the masculine is reinforced just in the form itself. It tends to reinforce the masculine side even of men. But then again as it's taught here it's much different than it's taught elsewhere.

R. Also there's a big difference between Rinzai and Sōtō. Some Rinzai monasteries are really quite overwhelmingly masculine. No woman in her right mind would want to go there.

Q. As a male doing Zen practice, I've found a growing tendency to be receptive or open.

R. That's good. When I first did sesshin in Japan at Engaku-ji, the temple at which Dr. Suzuki and Senzaki Sensei trained, the young monks were very curious about me. It was 1950 and maybe I was only the second or third foreigner that they'd seen in the monastery. One of them said to me during sesshin, "Have you gone in to fight with the Rōshi yet?" It took me a moment to realize that he was talking about dokusan. There is this spirit of confrontation in many of the Rinzai centers. The stronger the confrontation the better, it seems. You frequently would hear roaring, shouting, and angry words from the teacher's room. In all respect, I don't see how that can be the true Buddha Way. The extraordinary thing is that now and then you meet wonderful, compassionate, open men who emerged from that military training. They're not rough at all in their own teaching. Somehow they found their way, almost in spite of that macho atmosphere.

Q. It tends to happen with age.

R. Yes. I agree that it does happen with age, but it sometimes happens naturally or even as a result of that kind of training. Although I have not met him personally, I sense that Seikan Hasagawa is a sensitive and open person. He went through rigorous Rinzai training and wrote *The Cave of Poison Grass* when he was only thirty. But basically, Dōgen's dictum is fundamental. It is with the experience of other things that we find our interbeing.

Here I should be clear that interbeing is only one aspect of deepest experience. It is the Sambhogakāya, the most intimate harmony. Remember, there are two other aspects, the other two bodies of the Buddha: the Dharmakāya, the pure and clear void, and the Nirmānakāya, the unique individual. I have been using "interbeing" as a kind of shorthand for essential nature. However, it is expressive of only one aspect.

About experiencing things other than the self, it is superficially paradoxical that we must put ourselves out there so that we can be receptive, we have to come forth and ask—come forth and show—as we are. We have to put ourselves on the line. But there is a difference between putting myself on the line and insisting on a certain point of view in others.

Q. Is hearing the wind through the trees putting oneself on the line? Is that a feminine experience or a masculine experience?

R. It is indeed putting yourself on the line to hear the wind. You have to forget everything you have been conditioned to think of as something more important than wind. However, I don't know if it's feminine or masculine to do this. Another point is that just hearing the wind is not the ultimate position.

Keep your inquiring spirit. Remember Ch'ing-shui, putting himself on the line: "I am Ch'ing-shui, solitary and destitute. Won't you give me alms?"[17] Won't you help me? Here I am, as I am. What do you say, how do you treat me? A bit more feminine than masculine. No? At least in the way we think about female and male in our culture.

Q. I appreciate the fact that we're raising the questions about masculine and feminine. Let me just ask as a woman: Can you give us an example of how to encourage your will to be strong?

R. As I have suggested, the vows are one such good way and you can write your own. Look up the vows of Thich Nhat Hanh as examples. Their tradition has its source in the Pure Conduct chapter of the *Hua-yen ching*. You can consult my own gāthās in *The Dragon Who Never Sleeps*.[18]

You can make your own collection of sayings and verses that are reminders for you: for the intervals when you open the door, close the door, get into the car, get out of the car, pick up the hammer—there are countless opportunities. You can write down these turning points, cruxes, of your day. If you write all those occasions down, then you're more likely to remember them as you encounter them.

A second point is that it's important not to be discouraged at what you perceive as your failure of will. Resolve and will build with your practice of Right Recollection.

Q. I'd like to offer a personal experience that I've had with resolve. For many many years I was trying to find some way to integrate spiritual practice and work toward social change. I felt those two paths were separate. At some point it just clicked for me that I have to make spiritual practice the center of my life and go on from there to everything else. From that time on, back in 1981, everything was in place. That doesn't mean I haven't questioned this path or another path or questioned my own ability, but there was something very fundamental about my resolve at that point. It was a complete turnabout in my life. A couple of years later at a three-month retreat, in the midst of meditating, another resolve arose that was completely unconnected with myself. I didn't really know the Four Vows at the time, but if I had to put it into words, the resolve was, "Although the Buddha Way is endless, I vow to follow through." There was no doubt. It was like the resolve itself was going to follow through, it wasn't me.

So I learned that will isn't something that comes from the self. It comes from the nonself, if anything. And as you say, it's something that builds naturally. Even though we have to work on all these Pāramitās, they grow and develop as part of us and we don't even know it. Sometimes I turn around and look at myself and realize, "Aha, there's something different about the way I'm following through now than there was before." Almost like it snuck up on me. And so I see resolve as one of the most powerful aspects of practice in my own life.

R. You make it clear that resolve is an experience, vows made for you, as Wordsworth said. That takes the grimness out of practice, doesn't it? But tell me, how did your resolve affect your participation in social action?

Q. I got involved in social action with an attitude that was different than it was previously. I have always had a very combative attitude and even now I struggle with that on a daily basis. But I know there's this silent place underneath and beyond me and beyond practice and social action.

R. So there was actually not an overt difference in your life? You still participate in social action?

Q. Yes, though for the last few years I have been focusing on spiritual practice. I hesitate to act until I can come from a place of deeper understanding. I've acted much less and have focused more on teaching meditation. However, I've come to the point now where I know that when I return to Canada, it will be time to go back into the world.

Q. What is the connection between will and endurance?

R. Will and endurance are certainly intimately interconnected. One is the desire and the other is the follow-through. Let me give you an example from my own experience. Many years ago, I was in therapy. One of my problems was that I couldn't criticize anybody and I couldn't reject anything. Whatever came, came. I was very passive. My therapist assigned me a task. I was to go to a restaurant, order something, and then send it back. It was very difficult. I deliberately went to the next town where nobody knew me and even then it was hard. I was determined to follow through and I did it, though I confess I avoided that whole town afterward.

With the rising of resolve, practice is simply a matter of doing it, making it happen. Endurance or practice where there is no particularly deep incentive can really be pretty grim and difficult. But it might be necessary. Resolve builds. I had a lot more resolve to stand on my own feet after I was successful in bullying that poor waitress long ago. I wish now that I had had the gumption and decency to go back and take her some flowers.

Q. What about the resolve to quit smoking or to avoid overeating? These are very difficult addictions.

R. I have a dear friend who is making himself sick with smoking. It's to the point now where he can't say very much without coughing. So when I said good-bye to him recently, I said, "Stop smoking." And he said, "Yes, I'm going to have to. I can't breathe." It's that kind of awareness that's going to do it if anything is.

Q. Is there a difference between will toward something positive and will toward something negative?

R. Napoleon Hill wrote a book called *Think and Grow Rich.* It was in all the drugstores when I was a boy and is still in print. Compare this kind of will to Dōgen Zenji's words about Bodhichitta. It is not possible to earn wealth without study, or to realize the Buddha Way without practice. The person who has the mind-set and the intelligence can probably become wealthy or seduce somebody or rob a bank or whatever. Will is neutral and universal. So is Samādhi, incidentally. Samādhi is simply absorption. Absorption in what? Making money? So when you ask in this dōjō, "How can I cultivate will?" you are really asking something more particular, "How can I cultivate the will to realize essential nature?"

Remember that movie with Alec Guinness, *The Lavender Hill Mob*, where robbers conspire to pull off a big job? They dedicate all their energies to making it happen and all kinds of things happen to divert their efforts. They try to surmount the problems but eventually everything just falls apart. The whole movie is an exercise in group will. No matter what happens, even with cops pursuing them, they don't give up. They steal some gold and melt it down into little Eiffel Towers which are just like the little gilt Eiffel Towers that are sold as souvenirs. But by mistake one of them, just one of them, gets mixed up with the gilt ones and a little girl from England buys it. They trace that one little Eiffel Tower to the little girl in her school back in England, absolutely determined to get all the treasure, not just some of it. Ha ha!

We are caught up in that kind of pursuit, fueled with the same human energy. But you see, ours is fundamentally not a desire for personal wealth or attainment. Fundamentally it is a desire to be an avatar, to be a carrier, to be a messenger. Here is the next part of that chapter by Dōgen that I have been quoting:

> *You should not practice Buddha's teaching with the idea of gain. The practice of Buddha's teaching is always done by receiving the essential instructions of a master, not by following your own ideas. In fact, Buddha's teaching cannot be attained by having ideas or not having ideas. Only when the mind of pure practice coincides with the way will body and mind be calm. If body and mind are not yet calm, they will not be at ease. When body and mind are not at ease, thorns grow on the path of realization.*[19]

By "the mind of pure practice" Dōgen is talking about your original dwelling place, your home of peace, where there are no thoughts.

> *Clearly, Buddha-dharma is not practiced for one's own sake, and even less for the sake of fame and profit. Just for the sake of Buddha-dharma you should practice it.*
>
> *All Buddhas' compassion and sympathy for sentient beings are neither for their own sake nor for others. It is just the nature of Buddha-dharma. Isn't it apparent that insects and animals nurture their offspring, exhausting themselves with painful labors, yet in the end have no reward when their offspring are grown? In this way the compassion of small creatures for their offspring naturally resembles the thought of all Buddhas for sentient beings.*
>
> *The inconceivable dharma of all Buddhas is not compassion alone, but compassion is the basis of the various teachings that appear universally. Already we are children of the Buddhas. Why not follow their lead?*
>
> *Students! Do not practice Buddha-dharma for your own sake. Do not practice Buddha-dharma for name and gain. Do not practice Buddha-dharma to attain blissful reward. Do not practice Buddha-dharma to attain miraculous effects. Practice Buddha-dharma solely for the sake of Buddha-dharma. This is the way.*[20]

Q. What is the time period of these writings?

R. Early thirteenth century. It's part of the *Shōbō-genzō*, which is the large collection of some ninety-two talks by Dōgen Kigen, the founder of Sōtō Zen in Japan.

Q. So much of the literature is directed toward monks who are sitting a lot more than we lay-people are. The emphasis is on sitting as practice. I'd like to hear more about the rest of the day. Gāthās are fine when you are doing something that doesn't require all of your attention. . . .

R. On the one hand, when you are talking to someone, you are just talking with that person. When you are measuring, you are only measuring. When you are hammering, you are only hammering. When you are cooking, you are only cooking. On the other hand, as I said earlier, there are little hinges during your day, little points of change where you go from one thing to another. There's your chance. The moment you turn off the gas and turn to set the table there is a change in action—a point where you can remember.

Q. Normal cooking and cooking during sesshin are very different experiences. After cooking during the last sesshin, I know what it's like really to be present. It's a very good exercise in learning how to bring that presence, that mindful attention, to everyday acts.

R. Indeed.

Q. Is there a way that one can cook that is not practice? If you're cooking and thinking about something else, is that . . . ?

R. That's the common way—to have some kind of drama going in your head. It isn't practice. On the other hand, focusing just on the task in daily life is a kind of zazen. It is conducive to good zazen on your cushions.

Q. My problem is a daily schedule that is very busy. I have to get so many things done. To bring my mind back to the present moment I have to stop body movement and allow my thoughts to settle a bit. When you've got five things that you have to do, you just have to keep moving. I've found that it's very difficult to let the thoughts settle in that case.

R. It's difficult but I think it's good to practice it. When you put the phone down, breathe out. How much time are you losing there? Not very much. When you practice that diligently, you find that you're actually saving time because you're more settled.

Q. When you're just doing a single task, should you also be focusing on your practice?

R. If you're in the kitchen chopping, you have to pay attention to the chopping, otherwise you might chop your finger. If you are driving a car, you need to focus on all the details of driving. But if you diligently practice *Mu,* say, in intervals between tasks, then after a while, maybe months, maybe years, you will be moving around in the presence of *Mu* all day long, no matter what you are doing. It will be *Mu* chopping, *Mu* driving a car.

Q. Even when you haven't reached the presence of *Mu,* there are some things like sweeping the floor where you could follow your breath as you do it. Is that better than just sweeping?

R. This kind of minute distinction is something that you need to work out yourself. There are some people who would be just sweeping. There would be some people going "*Kan ji zai bo sa gyō . . .*"[21] as they sweep. And there are some people who would be breathing *Mu* as they sweep. This is what you work out yourself. When you do kinhin, what do you do, what's happening in your head? Think of sweeping and similar simple tasks as a kind of kinhin.

NINE

SPIRITUAL POWER

The Bala Pāramitā

Bala is spiritual or moral power or force. In his long Dharma poem, the *Cheng-tao ke*, Yung-chia encourages us to cultivate the Five Powers, the Pañchabala. These are traditionally: Faith (Shraddhā), Zeal (Vīrya), Recollection (Smirti), Absorption (Samādhi), and Wisdom (Prajñā).[1]

Like the Eightfold Path and the Ten Pāramitās, these Five Powers of the Bodhisattva are useful identifications of steps on the Path. Each step is perfection itself, but each gives notice of a different aspect of perfection.

Let me explicate these Five Powers: The Bala of Faith destroys doubt, the Bala of Zeal destroys sloth, the Bala of Recollection destroys false options, the Bala of Absorption destroys confused or wandering thoughts, and the Bala of Wisdom destroys the flat desert of self-centered preoccupation. Cultivate the Five Powers, cautions Yung-chia. Indeed.

These are the Bala of the Bodhisattva and—in this case—Bodhisattva means "one becoming realized." The Five Powers of the Bodhisattva are more or less self-explanatory, and it simply remains for us to build them step by step.

There are also Powers of the Buddha, the perfected one. But even the Buddha's perfection is still the perfection of practice, continually unfolding. There are ten of these Buddha practices and they seem by their phrasing to be out of reach. They really aren't. I will devote the rest of this essay to bringing them down to Earth.[2]

The First Power of the Buddha is "complete knowledge of right and wrong in all circumstances." "Right" does not have the same moral force in Buddhism that it does in Christianity and other religions originating in the Near East. It means "true"—in accord with reality, as opposed to delusory—untrue or "wrong."

You will recall how Ma-ku came to Chang-ching, carrying his bell staff. He circled Chang-ching's seat three times, brought the staff firmly to the floor, shaking the bells, and stood straight. Chang-ching said, "Right!" Ma-ku repeated the mime before Nan-ch'üan, but Nan-ch'üan said, "Not right!" When Ma-ku asked how come, Nan-ch'üan explained that Chang-ching was right, but Ma-ku was not.[3]

After all, the baby Buddha is said to have made a similar presentation, raising one hand and pointing to heaven, lowering the other and pointing to the Earth, while intoning, "Above the heavens, below the heavens, only I, alone and sacred." What would Nan-ch'üan have said to the baby Buddha? One of the first lessons I learned as a teacher of Zen Buddhism is that a student can give the "right" answer but still be mistaken.

To illustrate the importance of the Precept of Not Lying in *The Mind of Clover*, I gave the example of a father who lies about his child's age to save a few cents of bus fare, thereby destroying the child's sense of honesty.[4] It does more. The bus system of mutual interdependence requires a fare for every child over six. The father's responsibility to that system, as well as to his child's unique and particular person, requires that he give the right age for his child. When he tries to beat the system, he not only destroys his child's self-respect and innate sense of what is true, but he also tears at the fabric of the society that sustains him and his family.

The Second Power of the Buddha is "knowledge of the karma of every being, past, present, and future." We should understand about karma. It is not merely cause and effect, but affinity. Affinity is karma beyond the time line:

Punyamitra asked, "Do you remember past times or not?"

Prajñādhāra said, "I remember that in a far distant

kalpa I was living with you. You were preaching the Mahā-prajñā and I was reciting the deepest sūtras. The circumstances today are in accord with that ancient karma."[5]

Don't misunderstand. The circumstances today are in accord with ancient karma because those old times are the new times. We are living the old times today. Understanding this to the very bottom is "seeing into the karma of every being, past, present, and future."

In Japan you will frequently hear the expression "mysterious karma." This is an acknowledgment that we are all imperfect human beings and cannot understand fully the subtle workings of mutual interdependence across conventional time, "profane time," to use Mircea Eliade's term. The Fully Realized One sees more and more clearly into the affinities of each being. You and I can cultivate this kind of talent by encouraging our family members, friends, neighbors, co-workers, and indeed all people to pursue their own individual paths toward fulfillment. We can extend this encouragement to animals and plants as well, and to the Earth itself. As we watch individual people, animals, and plants mature, we take joy in their liberation from the obstacles that hindered them in former days and find affinity with their nature that is now flowering—no other than our own true nature in slightly different forms.

The Third Power is "the knowledge of all stages of Dhyāna and Samādhi." This would be our practice of zazen. Dhyāna is our posture or form on the cushions and more. As I indicated in Chapter 5, Dhyāna is also the ground of all the human virtues and is not merely grim concentration. Samādhi, a closely related condition, is the peaceful inner quality of zazen. And it is more as well, for that inner quality is the experience of interactive harmony with all beings. The other is no other than myself. That is the perfection of zazen.

At the same time, it is important to distinguish Dhyāna and Prajñā.

The Hermit of Lotus-Flower Peak held out his staff before his assembly and said, "Why didn't our Ancestors remain here when they reached it?" The assembly was silent.

Answering for them he responded, "It has no power for the journey."

Again he asked, "After all, what is it?" The assembly was again silent.

The Hermit said, "Carrying my staff across the back of my neck; going to the thousand, the ten-thousand peaks."[6]

I used to translate the Hermit's first response to himself as "It has no power for guidance." This is all right as far as it goes, but guidance is only one part of the journey. The word can also be translated "road," the dusty road of the Ganges Valley that the Buddha walked during his long teaching career, the dusty road of every Bodhisattva who has taken up the staff. But by itself the staff has no power. Concentration and absorption have no means for their own presentation. The Buddha reposed beneath the Bodhi tree with Dhyāna and Samādhi. With Prajñā he sought out and preached to his first five disciples in Benares.

Yün-men held out his staff before his assembly and said, "This staff has become a dragon. It has swallowed up the whole universe. Mountains, rivers, the great Earth—where can they be?"[7]

Exactly the same point. The Hermit of Lotus-Flower Peak shows where they could be, as if we didn't know every day of our lives, but he also shows us how we can deal with them. "Carrying my staff across the back of my neck, going to the thousand, the ten-thousand peaks." A delight!

The Fourth Power is "understanding the powers and faculties of all beings." This would be Yün-men's skill in dealing with students, Chao-chou's skill, Fa-yen's skill.

Chao-chou addressed his assembly and said, " 'The Supreme Way is not difficult: simply avoid picking and choosing.' With even a few words, 'this is choosing,' 'this is clarity.' This old monk does not dwell in clarity. Can you value this without reservation?"

A monk stepped forward and asked, "If you do not dwell in clarity, how can you value anything without reservation?"

Chao-chou said, "I don't know that either."

The monk asked, "If you don't know, how can you say that you do not dwell in clarity?"

Chao-chou said, "It is enough to ask about that matter. Make your bows and withdraw."[8]

The kōan portion of this case relates simply to Chao-chou's quotation from the *Hsin-hsin ming* (*Shinjinmei*, "Precepts of Faith in Mind"), another long Dharma poem, this one attributed to Seng-ts'an.[9] What is the Supreme Way in your daily life? What is not picking and choosing in your daily life? But you can appreciate also Chao-chou's understanding of the powers and faculties of the monk. A very clever fellow, it would seem, who needs to hold questions in mind instead of dissipating his inquiring spirit in such a flashy manner.

The Fifth Power is "the knowledge of the desires or moral direction of every being." This is a refinement of the understanding of the karma of everyone and everything and of their powers and faculties. In our mealtime sūtras we venerate "Shākyamuni, infinitely varied, Nirmānakāya Buddha."[10] We bow to the uniqueness of Shākyamuni and to the uniqueness of each being—but there is another step. We practice understanding of each being for and of itself, herself, himself. We practice understanding the potential of each being and the direction each being needs to take for maturity and fulfillment. With an open mind, the tendencies of others become clear. How can I encourage them?

The Sixth Power is "understanding the actual condition of

every being." This is not a matter of mind reading; that is to say it is not a matter of projecting yourself into the other. Quite the opposite, in fact. Seeing the actual condition of every being is a matter of forgetting yourself and being altogether open, of taking the other in with perfect reception through all the senses. This is not necessarily an act of approval, of course. The person is accepted; the words and conduct can thereby be evaluated in the context of shared weaknesses and strengths.

The Seventh Power is "understanding the direction and consequence of all laws." I am reminded of the ending of Case 38 of *The Blue Cliff Record,*

> *The Magistrate said, "The king's law and the Buddha's law have the same nature."*
>
> *Feng-hsüeh asked, "Why do you say that?"*
>
> *The Magistrate replied, "When called upon to judge, one must judge. Otherwise one invites disorder."*[11]

Making judgments is not always appropriate, but when it is called for, then it must be done. Sometimes you must cry out, "Stop that! That won't do!"

The Magistrate points to the ground that gives rise to the civil law on the one hand and Buddhist law on the other. It is also possible to point to the ground that gives rise to secular power and to power in the Buddhist sense. Order or harmony is the nature and function of civil and Buddhist law and of secular and Buddhist power. We tend to think of one as impure and the other as pure, but actually, even in our acquisitive society, the honest magistrate strives for order and harmony. Corruption may enter in, but the stars and the molecules sing on. The wise judge is thinking about this essential harmony, as is the Buddhist on the path of wisdom.

It is instructive to find that the word *Dharma* means "law" and that in Chinese the ideographs for "Dharma" and "civil law" are the same. The Chinese word *te* (Japanese: *toku*) means both "power" and "virtue."

The Eighth Power is "the complete knowledge of all causes of mortality and of good and evil in their reality." This would begin with a complete acceptance of my own lack of any permanent self and of the lack of anything permanent in the universe. "All things pass quickly away."[12] Understanding the causes of good action and bad action is clear insight into the wellsprings of ignorance and wisdom, exclusiveness and compassion. "Anguish is everywhere," as the Buddha said. Tormented by mortality and interdependence, the manager or the politician organizes in a vain effort to prove permanence and independent power. People suffer, animals suffer, plants suffer, seas suffer, the Earth suffers.

The source of good is, of course, freedom from self-centered anxieties. All one's energy is transmuted to loving-kindness, compassion, joy in the liberation of others, and equanimity. We delight in these Four Abodes among our friends and cultivate them secretly in our own conduct.

The Ninth Power is "understanding the end of all beings and Nirvāna." This would be knowing the nature of death and extinction. The end of all beings and Nirvāna are both relinquishment. Death is the final act of relinquishment, of Dāna, in this life. Whitman was, as Lewis Hyde points out, clear and profound on this point:

I bequeath myself to the dirt to grow from the grass I love,
If you want me again, look for me under your boot-soles.[13]

Death at the end of life is the metaphor, the equivalent of the Great Death in this life. This Great Death is no less the total relinquishment of absolutely everything. How does it happen? "Hear the cardinal! Hear the cardinal!" Everything else utterly disappears! Everything else is absolutely extinguished!

Finally, the Tenth Power of the Buddha, "the destruction of

illusion and delusion of every kind," is the practice of all the Ancestors.

Someone asked Chao-chou, "Where is your mind focused?"

Chao-chou replied, "Where there is no design."[14]

The sword that kills fixations and preoccupations becomes the sword that brings good-humored acceptance of life and death and good-humored sharing of the Way. This is my practice and yours. This is the Bala Pāramitā.

QUESTIONS AND RESPONSES

Q. Your example of the bus driver is very clear and simple. There's a rule and you obey it. If the rule isn't a good one, then is civil disobedience appropriate?

R. It's not so much that the father disobeyed a rule or the law. He violated the truth. He said something that wasn't so. The little boy didn't have to be told that you must tell the truth. He wasn't correcting his father on that basis. He was correcting his father on the basis of the fact "I am not five years old. I am six." When the Quakers say, "Speak truth to power," they are clearly implying that real power lies in the truth and that political expediency withers before it. Everybody knows, or senses at any rate, that if we don't stop relying on technological violence the planet Earth will perish. The emperor is exposed when such truth is brought forth. He is stark naked, just as we have known from the beginning.

Q. What about someone who feels impelled to blow up an abortion clinic because the truth is "Thou shalt not kill"?

R. The Devil quotes scripture and prisons and madhouses are full of people who hear voices telling them to do evil things. We can either wash our hands like Pilate, unable to identify truth, or we can inform ourselves, do our homework and our zazen and follow the teaching and the experience that are truly based on harmony and peace—as best we can. There is only one way to bring peace into the world and that is by being peace, showing peace, acting peace.

Anne Aitken and I are founding members of the Southern Poverty Law Center, which in the past few years has been following up and prosecuting members of the Ku Klux Klan. They have a publication called *Klanwatch.* A while back I wrote them a letter objecting to their confrontive and adversarial attitude toward members of the Klan. I didn't get an answer. However, perhaps because of my letter or because of a general change of attitude, they no longer use words like *ignorant rednecks* and *born losers* in their literature. I notice questions in their newsletter now, asking how can we reach such folks.

In my letter to *Klanwatch*, I pointed out they had prosecuted and gained the conviction of a nineteen-year-old man for shooting a policeman and killing him. His pickup truck was loaded with guns. He was stopped by the policeman. He panicked and shot the policeman. This young man was the son of a hard-bitten Klansman. When I reflect on myself at age nineteen, I recall that I was very much under the influence of my father and was just as militaristic as he was.

I am not saying that the Southern Poverty Law Center should not have urged prosecution of this young man for shooting a policeman, but the kid got life with no possibility of parole. Something's not quite right here. I am glad that the Center people are exposing the Klan for what it is. I'm glad that real criminals in the Klan are being prosecuted. But if we are really to follow the Buddha Dharma or the Christ Dharma, the law of the universe, we have to work out rigorous yet compassionate ways to help people to change. This kid should be confined harmlessly and encouraged to be harmless, however long that takes. But as a lifer in our American prison system, with no possibility of parole, he is sure to be reached by the Aryan Brotherhood, sure to receive reinforcement for the views that he had when he was nineteen. There is no hope for him, I suppose.

Q. Regarding the Second Power of the Buddha, knowledge of the karma of every being, past, present, and future: Certain sūtras talk about the Buddha being able to see the past lives of every individual. Hasn't that power disappeared from Zen?

R. Whether there actually are such sūtras or not I can't say. I am not familiar enough with the literature. But you are right that very little, if anything, is said about past lives in Zen, except to show that we are living them now.

I'll never forget the time when another speaker and I made presentations to a class at the Kapiolani Community College. The two of us had different points of view. She made her presentation first, and it consisted entirely of reading the past lives of students in the room—this one was a princess on the Nile, that one a gladiator in Rome, and so on. I was sitting in the back of the room, probably with a very skeptical expression on my face. She didn't dare identify my past lives. In fact, she said, "I see someone back there who is looking rather doubtful." *Doubtful* is hardly a strong enough word.

Q. Is your interpretation of these powers a classical Zen interpretation or is it your own? When you first read them, they sounded like a yogic training school. It seems like people studying Yoga would use them literally to figure out all the aspects of everything.

R. They are the classic Buddhist interpretation, which I am using as my own. When you make such teachings your own, they become soft and flexible. You understand that there is nothing completely absolute and nothing completely relative. You find that each act on the path of perfection is perfection itself. That is to say, each point in the sequence is the absolute. But I hasten to point out that the opposite is also true. You cannot subtract the sequence from the immediate. You cannot subtract the temporal from the eternal. You cannot subtract karma from the essential. When all this is internalized, it is most naturally taught in the form of folk stories: the Jātaka Tales in Classical Buddhism, the kōans in Zen.

Look again at Case 2 of the *Wu-men Kuan* where an old man comes in to hear Pai-chang give teishōs and then leaves with the monks each time. One day he remains behind. Their conversation goes like this:

> *Pai-chang asked, "Who are you, standing here before me?"*
>
> *The old man said, "Indeed, I'm not a human being. In the far distant past, in the days of Kāshyapa Buddha"* [that is to say, in the days before Shākyamuni Buddha], *"I was head monk at this mountain. One day, a monk asked me, 'Does the person of complete realization fall under the law of cause and effect or not?' I replied, 'Such a person does not fall under the law of cause and effect.' With this I was reborn five hundred times as a fox. I beg you to give me a turning word to release me from my lives as a fox. Tell me, does the person of complete realization fall under the law of cause and effect or not?"*
>
> *Pai-chang said, "Such a person does not evade the law of cause and effect."*[15]

Another translation is "Such a person is not blind to the law of cause and effect." The old man was promptly enlightened and the story goes on, but this is enough for our purposes.

This is a very interesting kōan, a very interesting and instructive folk story. The old man was also Pai-Chang. Pai-chang was the name of the mountain; the head priest is named after the mountain, so there are a whole series of Pai-changs going on back through time. So here is Pai-chang teaching himself, you might say.

From the very beginning in Buddhism it has been said that your task is to purify yourself so that there is no residue left to be reborn. The old man wasn't incorrect from that point of view. Then how is it that he was reborn five hundred times as a fox? That wasn't retribution. Don't suppose that there is some bearded old fellow up there who declares, "Oh oh, you made a mistake, so this is your punishment!"

It's not incorrect to say that such a person does not fall under the law of cause and effect. It is not incorrect to say that we attain perfectly. In *The Gateless Barrier* I tell about the time Kalu Rinpoché came to Maui many years ago. All of us from the Maui Zendō went to hear him. During the question period, a young man stood up and asked, "Does the person of complete realization fall under the law of cause and effect or not?" Kalu Rinpoché said, "Such a person does not fall under the law of cause and effect."

For Kalu Rinpoché the person of complete realization is no longer human in the ordinary sense and has no further need to practice. This is a valid position, but it can also be a trap for teachers and students alike. When the teacher acts out somehow, the students say, "Oh, he's testing us!" instead of saying, "What a bad teacher!" The mature Pai-chang is saying, in effect, there is perfection and then there is perfection again. And perfection again.

Q. So instead of using the word *perfection* you might use the word *perfecting*.

R. Yes, but that dampens it. It softens it. It puts the matter exclusively on the karmic side. It is better to say "perfection," I think. It contains both meanings and is properly ambiguous. Is there such a thing as an unambiguous truth? There's a mine field for you!

Kalu Rinpoché was right, after all, just as the old Pai-chang was right. If we fall into the attitude that there is merely karma, then we err on that side. In his poem to this case, Wu-men says, "Not evading, not falling; a thousand mistakes, ten thousand mistakes." There are two sides here and you can fall into error on either side. You fall into error if you postulate an endless process of fate. You fall into error if you presume there is a be-all and an end-all kind of liberation. The be-all and end-all and the endless process are one and the same. They can't be separated. So you need a word that implies both process and completion. And that word is *perfection.*

Q. So is that the relationship between causality and affinity?

R. Yes, that's it. It is not merely a relationship. Just as the two Pai-changs were the same person, so causality and affinity are the same. In the concrete language of Theravāda Buddhism, when you say "This happens because that happens," you are also saying "This is because that is." Time and no time are the same.

Q. In that case, why have so much doubt about past lives and future lives?

R. Who doubts? That is a much more fundamental question.

Q. How is it that people say that Shākyamuni was a perfectly realized being? Causality accounts for facts like he died of poisoned mushrooms or something.

R. It's all right to say that Shākyamuni was perfectly accomplished. His practice of perfection is so close to the state of absolute perfection that there is very little to identify as imperfect. But at the same time he was and is a human being. He did not walk on water and these days he would have to be careful crossing the street.

This brings to mind the discussion of perfectionism we had a while back.[16] Even the perfectionistic person needs to shift only a tiny bit to be a wonderful student—only a tiny bit because the ideal is there, the lamp is there. It just needs trimming and lighting. Many parents have to cope with perfectionism in their children. In fact, perfectionism is a childish trait. It is very normal in children. "I can't do it so I won't try. It's too hard for me."

Q. Or they'll spend hours doing it and redoing it.

R. Yes. I can hear my own parents saying to me that it's all right to have blots on my letter to my grandmother. "She'll understand," they would say. Well, I didn't want her to understand that I was imperfect. I wanted to write a nice letter.

Q. How does this develop the point that a perfectly realized person appears to be subject to the law of cause and effect?

R. Perfection is both a process and a state. To be as perfect as possible, as Yamada Rōshi said, is a wonderful aspiration. But this little tiny tail, what a wonderful thing it is. This tail of humanity doesn't go through the window ever.[17]

Q. I'd like to get back to power. I was thinking about Abou Ben Adhem and our role as empowered human beings.

R. I think Abou Ben Adhem is a great example. Can you recite it for us?

Q. *Abou Ben Adhem (may his tribe increase!)*
Awoke one night from a deep dream of peace,
And saw, within the moonlight in his room,
Making it rich, and like a lily in bloom,
An angel writing in a book of gold:—
Exceeding peace had made Ben Adhem bold,
And to the presence in the room he said,
"What writest thou?"—The vision rais'd its head
And with a look made of all sweet accord,
Answered, "The names of those who love the Lord."
"And is mine one?" said Abou. "Nay, not so,"
Replied the angel. Abou spoke more low,
But cheerily still; and said, "I pray thee then,
Write me as one who loves his fellow men."

The angel wrote and vanished. The next night
it came again with a great awakening light
and show'd the Book of Names whom love of God had bless'd,
And lo! Abou Ben Adhem's name led all the rest.[18]

R. Yes, that's right. Wonderful. It is not clear why Abou was not included in the book the first night. In fact, it seems that Leigh Hunt is expressing a shift from confusion about just what the love of God really means to the understanding that it is a love of humanity that is, after all, the touchstone of religious salvation. It seems that this is in keeping with a new sense of personal responsibility for religious practice that was evolving in the Romantic Period. The second night it was as though God had finally gotten clear about the matter himself. "That's it!"—and he put Abou at the head of the list. Abou's voice lowered with his awareness of the momentous nature of the shift, and he was cheered by it. We suffer with all others, not just with a single savior. We ourselves are empowered as saviors, a role we can only accept modestly, like Abou Ben Adhem, because we know that there is nothing enduring or substantial here within us. The universe is freed to grow through us, as it grows through lima beans.

Q. There is also the point that empowerment and responsibility can be encouraged. I respond to someone who sees in me what I would like to be. I think all of us have had that experience, as well as the reverse.

R. Yes. It is a confirmation, helping you own your potential and to realize it in your thoughts and conduct. Our Jukai ceremony is a ritual of helping students to own their personal ideals. In preparing for Jukai I ask people to write me a little letter outlining their aspirations—what they would like themselves to be. From there I get an idea for a good name for them. We consult and agree upon a name. I then inscribe that name on their rakusu, the garment they wear for all rituals including zazen, that represents the Buddha's robe. When they don the rakusu, they don the Buddha's robe, of course, but they also take on the name that expresses their highest ideals, the name they have made their own. "That's me," they can say.

If that is encouraging and an act of teaching, then the opposite is very destructive: "You are useless." "You are lazy." "You are dumb." When people change their first names the chances are that Mom or Dad is constantly in their heads saying something like, "Earline, you idiot!" So Earline becomes Stephanie.

Q. You wrote something recently to the effect that your role as a teacher is to encourage.

R. Yes, that is the only possible role, the only possible use of power. I may see to some degree into the faculties of students, their desires and moral directions, their actual condition, and so on. These are aspects of character that a person can cultivate to her or his own maturity and fulfillment. I want to encourage the positive in these qualities.

Some Zen teachers tend to be rather naive in their view of other people, not seeing the bad, not being aware of the mistakes and tendencies to be disorganizing or disruptive or malicious or anything like that. This was particularly true of Sōen Rōshi who to the end of his life was a complete innocent. He was naturally innocent, always wanting to bring forth the Bodhisattva. But surely this is a fault on the right side of the ledger. The put-down can only be destructive. Damning with faint praise can only be destructive.

Q. I can't help but feel that maybe we should rewrite these Ten Powers in a way that really works for us. These categories really seem distant for me, not quite fleshy. They don't really seem to hit home.

R. How about this discussion? Has it hit home? I see these classical categories as latticework. We train ourselves on them. I agree with you that we can't simply leave them as a cold structure. But it's very useful to get at just what karma is, what Dhyāna and Samādhi are, how each of us has individual tendencies and a set of interests. You and I come together as individual entities because there are elements that make us up that have their affinities. The interests and the affinities of those interests have put together our liver, our lungs, our brain, and all of those things, down to the most minute points in our genes. It is all contained here in this body, in that body. The qualities and tendencies and interests and their affinities are the eggs, so to speak, the seeds for our maturity.

Q. I'm not very clear about the notion of power. When I'm doing zazen, when I'm settled in my mind, I feel that I have a kind of personal power. It seems that the world comes toward me. Now, I try not to make anything out of it. . . .

R. Don't be afraid of power or the word *power.* When you forget yourself, the world does indeed come to you. Responsibility enters here. The Five Powers of the Bodhisattva and the Ten Powers of the Buddha are powers of wisdom and compassion. You notice the miracle of things coming together and working out. Your power and universal power are in harmony when your mind is empty.

Q. I still feel uneasy. It seems to me that there is a fine line between the natural power of zazen and the power that is arrogant and exploitive.

R. It may seem to be a fine line when judged from outside, but experientially the two conditions are on opposite sides of the world. They are different worlds. The natural power of zazen is the power of the universe, soil, seed, wind, rain, thrusting up through lima beans into the air. The beans have been given their power, and they give their power back to the universe and enrich it in turn. On the other hand, the act of gathering universal riches to oneself is arrogant power. Soil, wind, rain, animals, and other people are used up and the universe is impoverished.

When you sense your power of zazen and realization, your mind naturally turns to your fellow beings, as the Buddha's mind turned to his five disciples in Benares. He knew very well what he could do in the world. But we don't get any hint in the sūtras of arrogance or self-concern on his part. On the other hand, if you don't feel such authority you are paralyzed. Perhaps you should remain under the Bodhi tree a bit longer. But don't delude yourself. Your confidence might just be waiting there to be confirmed.

Q. The other night I had an experience in bed. I had a visitor. I woke up in the morning and wrote a little poem: "Even in the darkest of the night he moves freely, but my teacher strictly warns me against talking about miraculous powers." And then I drew a picture of this cockroach. Now, you said something earlier about when the universe imposes itself on the self, that's enlightenment. That word *impose*—the cockroach didn't impose itself on me at all. There he was.

R. *Impose* is not the right word, but I see your point.

Q. I don't know what the right word is.

R. "Confirms the self," that's what Dōgen said. That's what the cockroach did.

TEN

KNOWLEDGE

The Jñāna Pāramitā

Jñāna means "knowledge" and *Prajñā* means "wisdom." The two words are often confused, for they are alike in pronunciation and meaning. Indeed, "knowledge" can mean "wisdom," even in the deepest sense, and the reverse is also true.

Several years ago, some of us from the Maui Zendō visited Kahoʻolawe, an island sacred to the Hawaiian people that had been used for decades as a bombing target by the U.S. Navy. We had informal seminars with Hawaiian leaders, including Uncle Harry Mitchell, a *kupuna* or elder, who guided us through some of the basics of Hawaiian religion. In his talk he emphasized the importance of "knowledge." I remember him repeating, "Knowledge! You know what I mean, knowledge!" It was quite a humorous talk. "I only went third grade, you know," he would say, by way of explaining that by "knowledge" he did not mean book knowledge but wisdom. Yet he meant "knowledge" too.

The two terms are potent when used together. In Chinese they are found in a compound, "wisdom/knowledge," that synthesizes the meanings. However, the old teachers also distinguished Jñāna from Prajñā. In this essay that is my purpose as well.

Jñāna is the Tenth and last Pāramitā and Dāna, giving, is the first. We have seen how Dāna is basically relinquishment and how this first step leads to all others. Jñāna as the last step is a kind of summing up, a knowledge of all the Perfections, and indeed of the many Upāya, the countless ways of cultivating perfection.

All this might seem rather intellectual and indeed it requires a clear, sound intellect for its comprehension. At the same time, the Perfection of Knowledge is not a matter simply of assimilating information. When I was in college, one of my friends remarked that professors teach us what we already know. This has always been the practice of instruction. Notice the structure of religious manuals written in India. Each point is made with a reference to common experience. Each point skillfully shows us the path that is beneath our feet.

This common experience is expressed in Zen Buddhism more personally and intimately than could be possible through philosophy or metaphysics. In Zen literature and in the dokusan room the presentation is the experience itself, reenacted in drama or mime as the living fact. Most of us distinguish play from ordinary communication. We attend plays and concerts as special events and otherwise reserve the word *play* for the activity of children or for adult recreation. The child plays on the floor, pushing a toy train and calling out, "Toot toot!" We smile patronizingly. But the child fuels the train, as I made the water go down the spout when I dared to twirl around at a class.[1] I could have called out, "Gurgle gurgle!" and the presentation would have been more effective.

The Jñāna Pāramitā is concerned with understanding such Upāya. "Gurgle gurgle" is onomatopoeia. The Japanese language is unusual in its inclusion of onomatopoeia in adult language. There are literally thousands of examples. For instance, I know of three onomatopoeic words for the quality of rain: *pita-pita* for a sprinkle, *pata-pata* for a shower, and *zā-zā* for a downpour. There are probably many more. Japanese adults use these words with a smile, quite conscious of their childish appeal, finding intimacy with the rain and with each other.

All words and phrases were originally intimate with experience but many have lost their intimacy, which is to say they have lost their meaning. They have lost their freight and are just deadheading. The phrase "rosy cheeks," for example, dropped its roses long ago. Other words and phrases have cargo that is directed elsewhere. When I look up a word in the dictionary, I find its definition all right, but unless it is addressed within my intellectual sphere—or just beyond it so that my sphere is enlarged—then I can't retain it, or I misunderstand and misuse it. Many years ago, I wrote the autobiographical piece "Willy-nilly Zen."[2] My Japanese friends had a hard time understanding what I meant by "willy-nilly." I had a hard time explaining. Then one day on rereading *Walden*, I found Thoreau separating the term, "will-ye nil-ye," and there it was: "Whether you want to or not." All that time, even using the term in the title of an essay, I had only a general idea of its meaning. Thoreau showed me how the freight of the term was my own treasure. Incidentally, it was there in the dictionary, just waiting for me to look it up.

Basically, words and phrases are archetypes. I have been holding a discussion by correspondence with a friend who prefers the term "the way of enlightenment" to the term "Buddha Way" in the last line of the "Great Vows for All."[3] Our translation of the Great Vows gāthā is problematic but I think "Buddha Way" is better than "the way of enlightenment." In a recent letter I remarked at one point: "I feel that archetypes are to some extent conditioned. The being of Kuan-yin, or Mary, or whatever, is there from the beginning in the human psyche in an inchoate form. It is the name that gives the inchoate being definition and brings it forth. The more specific the name, the sharper the definition and the clearer the presentation."

It is for this reason, more or less consciously, that I persist in using "zazen" rather than "meditation," "Bodhisattva" rather than "Enlightening Being," "sesshin" rather than "retreat," "Dharma" rather than "teaching," and most important of all, "*Mu*" rather than "No." I don't merely feel that these words should be naturalized as English words. More than that. They are archetypes, loaded with valuable ore that is lost when they are rendered in an explanatory manner. The "way of enlightenment" is not the Buddha's Way.

Many years ago, Senzaki Nyogen Sensei wrote a weekly column in the *Rafu Shimpō*, the Japanese-language newspaper of

Los Angeles. Each column was a commentary on a single Chinese ideograph. A column of this kind could also be done with English words such as *atonement* or *redemption* or *decency* or *conscience.* Each word or phrase, even "rosy cheeks" as the original metaphor, is a hologram charged with the universe. Each word or phrase can be an *arcanum.*

The arcanum is a concentrated metaphor, a tarot card, for example, that holds within itself profound revelations about human nature and about the essential nature of the universe. This archetypal metaphor can be encouraged to reveal itself only with patient, exacting meditation. *Mu* is the ultimate arcanum.

After hearing my talk on the Jñāna Pāramitā, one of my correspondents commented in a letter: "A true symbol is enigmatic and intriguing or else it no longer is one. It points beyond itself to a reality that cannot be expressed or grasped otherwise. It appears, mystifies, somehow leads onwards. That is its power. Once it is allegory or just a logo (i.e., "this" means "that") it loses its function of transformation."[4]

Which is to say, some things are far more powerful than others in guiding the human spirit. Words and phrases on a billboard or in TV advertising will only very occasionally and accidentally say anything that is potentially important to the serious pilgrim. But some words and phrases, or nearly any word or phrase at a particular time, can be the Tao of the Buddha. Remember the story I cited earlier about T'ou-tzu and the monk who asked about the voices of the Buddha: "Are all voices the voices of the Buddha?" "Yes indeed." "How about the voice of your rear end?" *Whack*! Not that time![5]

Dōgen Zenji said, "Words and phrases liberate discriminating thought."[6] Certain words and phrases can liberate the human mind from its tendency to turn back upon itself and fall into philosophical or psychological speculation. *Mu,* for example, can liberate the human mind from such questions as "Who is meditating on *Mu*?" or "What is the process of meditating on *Mu*?"

Notice that Dōgen Zenji does say not that words and

phrases kill and give life, after the manner of Wu-men and other Chinese masters. The human mind, the no-mind of the universe, does not come into being or go out of being. It is liberated only in the sense that we experience liberation when *Mu*, for example, becomes clear to us. The words and phrases turn the Dharma Wheel for us and help us to see what is already there and to acknowledge it consciously as our own.

Here I'd like to return to a point I passed over earlier. I said that archetypes can be conditioned to a certain extent. Nowhere is this more evident than in kōan study. To take a familiar example:

> *Yang-shan asked a monk, "Where have you just come from?"*
>
> *The monk said, "Lu Mountain."*
>
> *Yang-shan said, "Did you visit Five Elders Peak?"*
>
> *The monk said, "No, I didn't get there."*
>
> *Yang-shan said, "Then you never visited the mountain at all."*
>
> *Yün-men said, "These words were spoken out of benevolence and thus they fell into grasses."*[7]

This case is loaded with metaphors—archetypal words and phrases. "Where have you just come from?" will seem like an ordinary question, and indeed it can be. But hidden in the words is an inquiry into the monk's realization, "In this world of coming and going, where do you stand?" Without some experience, the inner significance of Yang-shan's question would be missed.

The monk then replies, "Lu Mountain." This might be an ordinary reply, indicating where the monk had been recently on pilgrimage, or it might be a temporizing reply—"Let's see what the Old Boss will say next." It might even be a reply out of deep understanding. The meaning of *Lu* is "Hermitage," so "Hermitage Mountain" is where the monk was most recently.

The word *mountain* is always charged with power in the context of Buddhism. Yang-shan's own name means "Appropriate Mountain." Each monastery has a mountain name. Ryūtaku-ji, where I trained, was "Entsū-san," or "Mountain of Complete Passage."

"Did you go to Five Elders Peak?" Yang-shan asks. "Well, I'm not sure if you know about mountains," Yang-shan is implying. "Let's see if you have been to the peak." It turns out that the monk hasn't and Yang-shan says, in effect, that he must take another step. Then later Yün-men sticks his oar in. To get his ironic point, we need to understand that "grasses" are the weeds of confusion.

Kōan study is a matter of making an old story our very own. It involves seeing into the wording to the bottom, to the ground of essential nature. It involves making words intimate in the context of a story—such words as *mountain, gate, cloud, dew, thunder, lightning, tiger, grasses, robber, path, old, white, black, near and far, come and go.* How would you respond to Yang-shan's question—"Did you go to Five Elders Peak?"

The names of the personages in the Zen Buddhist pantheon also have roles in the Jñāna Pāramitā—Mañjushrī, Samantabhadra, Kuan-yin—there are many. They are woven into a tapestry of spiritual culture from which our practice emerges. Understanding this tapestry is a matter of assimilation, rather than translation into our own figures of speech. Our task is to discern the patterns, colors, texture, composition, and significance within their realm and to make them our own.

I have sometimes come away from a talk on Zen Buddhist practice with the feeling that I might this time have conveyed some of the Tathāgata's true meaning—only to have a student say something like "I enjoyed your talk, but I didn't understand a word you said." It takes a while to assimilate the metaphors and the attitude.

The easiest way to begin this assimilation is with Chinese poetry. Here is Po Chü-i, perhaps the greatest of the T'ang period poets:

I take your poems in my hand and read them beside the candle;
The poems are finished, the candle is low, dawn not yet come.
With sore eyes by the guttering candle, still I sit in the dark,
Listening to waves that driven by the wind strike the prow of the boat.[8]

Here's another, this one by Tao Yüan-ming:

Swiftly the years, beyond recall,
Solemn the stillness of this fair morning.
I will clothe myself in spring-clothing,
And visit the slopes of the Eastern Hill.
By the mountain-stream a mist hovers,
Hovers a moment, then scatters.
Here comes a wind blowing from the south
That brushes the fields of new corn.[9]

Straightforward poems, you might feel. Zen Buddhism is straightforward too, and if you find the ground of Po Chü-i and Tao Yüan-ming, you have found the ground of Zen. Find the ground of Bashō and Buson, and you have found the ground of Zen. There are many names for this ground. Yün-men called it the light, Huang-po called it the mind, P'an-shan asks where it is:

P'an-shan said, "In the three worlds, there is no Dharma. Where shall we search for the mind?"[10]

All right, old man P'an-shan, I make my bows and acknowledge your wisdom. But I'd rather take tea and enjoy the lifting of the mountain mist with Tao Yüan-ming.

QUESTIONS AND RESPONSES

Q. Did you say that if a person genuinely wants to understand Buddhism she needs to take up Chinese poetry?

R. I said that perhaps a good way to begin getting a picture of the tapestry of Asian culture is to read Chinese poetry. I think Chinese poetry is the most accessible of all of Asian literature. It's more accessible than Haiku really. I'm old and stuck in my preferences and think that Arthur Waley, the translator of the two poems that I read, is still one of the really great translators of Chinese poetry. His books are still available and they are delightful. Unconsciously you get a sense of the tapestry by reading his work.

Q. It's ethnocentric of me, but I have a very difficult time understanding or seeing into the simplicity of the poems that you've read. Instead, I hear the form and the rhythms of European classics. I don't know what the form is. I can't read the pictographs.

R. The Chinese ideograph was originally a pictograph, but evolved from that form thousands of years ago. It's not consistently an *idea*-graph either, though that's as close a word as we have to describe it. Waley's method was to give the English line the same number of beats that it had in the Chinese. So that's the form.

Q. When I look at the Chinese characters, there's a block. They seem so different from anything I'm used to.

R. I don't think that it's really possible for a beginner in the Chinese language to get much out of Chinese poetry in the original, picking out each character laboriously in the dictionary and so on. So for those who don't intend to become serious students of Chinese, maybe it's enough just to listen to the English words in the translation.

Q. Thinking about archetypes, there should be no reason for my humanity to stop on English shores.

R. That's the discussion I'm having with my friend who wants to translate "Buddha's Way" as "the way of enlightenment." The position of my colleague is that archetypes can't be learned. My position is that they can, that, for example, we all share an unformed notion of mercy. We may not give it a name. But when we do name it, say, Kuan-yin, then it has pungency and shape and power.

Q. Recently I'm influenced by Robert Graves, who criticized the terms Carl Jung used. Graves says that it's not right to say that in our culture we have grown from our past, from little childish creeps into sophisticated people.

R. That's interesting. Primal people were and are not little childish creeps. Nonetheless, I admire Jung. He is the one who made an archetype out of archetypes, so to speak. When he spoke of the dream symbols such as the wise old woman, the dwarf, and so on, he was bringing certain inchoate tendencies into dream forms.

Q. A couple of things: First of all, I used to sit with a group related to this one that used that very phrase "The way of enlightenment is beyond attainment," or something like that. I felt quite relieved when I got here and found people saying "Buddha's Way." It seems much more connected and personalized. The other way sets you adrift. Where do Dōgen and Bodhidharma and all those people fit in if you just say "the way of enlightenment"?

R. Yes, when you follow the Buddha's Way, then you are encouraged to read and practice and experience yourself in the lineage.

Q. Which takes me to the other point, reading. The old man you mentioned on Kahoʻolawe said you need knowledge. He said, "I have a third-grade education," and he talked about knowledge. Here's a person you're praising and yet, in your primer on Zen, you have a list of books that you recommend. Every year you come out with a new booklist. In my average day I am so stressed out, so wrought up emotionally and mentally, that I go to bed at night and I can do nothing but go to bed. I can't read! Or if I read, it's some stupid science fiction novel or something.

R. Okay. I love Uncle Harry but he is his own man in every way. When he talked about knowledge, he was not recommending that you read anything and I'm not about to recommend that *he* read anything. He can do his own work. But those of us who find ourselves on the Zen Buddhist path can find it very helpful to read. Reading brings the kind of understanding that can prompt the knowledge that Uncle Harry was talking about. If you find yourself stressed out, I think it would be important to take yourself in hand anyway—and I'm talking to myself as well as to you. Take down the book that you want to read and read it for ten minutes. Read it out loud, if that helps.

Q. I'd like to talk a little bit more about poetry and Zen. It seems to me that poets—people who are sensitive to words, Eastern or Western—have something in common. When I read Chinese poets and when I read some twentieth-century poets, I find they're inhabiting the same world. There's a process going on that is the same. But do you suppose that grows just out of that attention to the language? Or does it have to connect with something deeper? I find Zen literature to be poetical, even though it is mostly prose, mostly conversation.

R. Well, the language of Zen and the language of poetry are similar in that both are presentational. In Susanne Langer's scheme there are two kinds of expression in the world, presentational and discursive.[11] "Buddha's Way" would be presentational, "the way of enlightenment" discursive. I find Chinese poetry to be like the poetry of John Clare, the early-nineteenth-century British pastoral poet: "Little trotty wagtail he goes in the rain"—but even plainer and somehow more pure. However, there's the question hovering in modern Western poetry, "What is the process of my poems?"—a preoccupation with the self.

Q. I recognize that, but I was thinking about this Pāramitā and the fact that we've talked about it in terms of words and phrases. Though there's a difference in posture and direction and intention in some of the Western poetry, still the poet has put his heart to school. He's careful about words, he's concerned about words, he's concerned about the world that he builds with those words. Because of that a note has been struck, or there's music, or there's an opening that wasn't there before. And so, though much of it doesn't have the tone of Chinese poetry, or should I say, is superficially ordinary speech, still, much of it strikes very deep.

R. Do you know Case 86 in *The Blue Cliff Record*?

> *Yün-men addressed his assembly and said, "Each of you has your own light. If you try to see it, you can't. The darkness is dark, dark. Now, where is your light?" Answering for them, he said, "The storeroom. The gate."*[12]

This is a rather bald expression of what both Po Chü-i and Tao Yüan-ming were expressing. That is where the light comes. And then there is the matter of words as words.

Q. You mentioned the phrase "Willy-nilly," which, if I understood it correctly, means "Will you or will you not."

R. "Will ye or nil ye." *Nil* means "not." Whether you will or not, in other words. It means I do it whether I want to or not.

Q. Okay. This brings me to my question about resistance to practice. It seems that there are two forces operating, one the force of desire, or wanting to become, and the other is an incentive to negate. In either case I don't think forcing works over the long run.

R. This is pertinent, because the Jñāna Pāramitā is a matter of knowing about Upāya, not just words of Upāya, but action too. The important thing is not to worry about resistance. If you and I were free of resistance, we would both of us be enlightened at this moment. It is resistance that prevented the Buddha from being enlightened as soon as he sat down under the Bodhi tree. The reason that you have resistance is that you share the nature of the Buddha Shākyamuni. We all have this human nature, so it's all right. Be easy with it, because if you push it, it's going to push back. So you can bargain with it lightly. Deal with it lightly. If you think you should come to sesshin, choose a nice short sesshin to begin with. Or come part-time. Lots of people come part-time. Nobody asks you what you're doing the other part of your time. You might be going to the beach. That's okay. Gradually, gradually, let your determination build.

Q. What makes it build?

R. That's the mystery. It happens not only in Zen practice but in any kind of endeavor. Count your blessings and let it evolve.

Q. Talking about archetypes, I notice that during dokusan you tend to be very quiet. I am puzzled about the archetype you show of being silent and holding back. Are you drawing the student forward? How does that work? Could you speak about that?

R. It's not so purposeful, you know. . . .

Q. Did I say it was?

R. No, indeed. That was by way of introducing the fact that I'm having difficulty saying anything about it. I'm eager to hear. I'm eager to see. So I keep quiet.

Q. At what point do you look at the person? When I come to dokusan, we make eye contact at the moment when I raise my head. You don't look at me when I first come in—or do you?

R. Oh, I look at you when you're bowing, of course.

Q. When I enter through the door, can you see me there?

R. Not the outside door; it's out of my line of sight. I see you when you enter the inner door.

Q. I had a definite feeling that you were away.

R. Oh no, I like to see how this bow goes and how that bow goes.

Q. I see. And so it isn't that you turn on at the moment when the person is ready.

R. Oh no, I like to see. I may do a bit of zazen in between, but when somebody appears at the door—[claps] *"I'm ready!"*

Q. I know that you see the exits. I wasn't so sure about the entrances.

R. You can be sure. I'm also listening to the steps. When we move to Pālolo, everybody will ring the kanshō bell before they come, and I'll listen to that too. We don't ring it here at Koko An out of consideration for our neighbors.

Q. When you listen to the bell, what do you hear?

R. I hear someone who is measured, I hear someone who is hurried, I hear someone who is anxious, I hear someone who is angry.

Q. Rōshi, a number of years ago, when I was on the Buddhist Peace Fellowship Board, there was a suggestion that we take the references to Buddhism out of our statement of purpose—you know, to take out "Buddha Way" and substitute "Dharma"—or maybe change it to "Truth" or something like that. I opposed it then, although I could see the reasoning that if we identify ourselves as Buddhist then we are setting up divisions. In *Turning Wheel*, the Buddhist Peace Fellowship (BPF) journal, there was an article by Toni Packer not long ago that said something similar. This goes back to the earlier discussion.

If you speak of "Truth," it's a free-floating thing that's not connected anywhere. If you say "Buddha Way," it gives you a place, it gives you a ground, a history. But I want to ask you to speak about the tension between those two positions, between wanting to be universal and yet be grounded in one's history and particular place.

R. Of course this is a problem that I face as a teacher and a writer and as one who encourages Sangha growth. When I turned in a recent manuscript to the publisher I was rather appalled at the length of my glossary. I would like to find the middle way here but I don't really have one foot in each camp, you know. I have maybe one and one half feet in the traditional camp. Words are teachers. "To touch the mind" is the meaning of *sesshin*, a marvelous meaning, so "retreat" just won't do as a translation. I want to be mindful of these questions that Toni Packer and others are raising and to examine my vocabulary in that light. However, I confess that I do so from the position that it's important to keep those words that are really teachers.

Look at *Dharma*, for example. There are three main meanings of this term. One is a reference to the Dharmakāya, the infinite emptiness, empty infinity that is charged with possibilities. The second meaning refers to the Sambhogakāya, karma and affinity—the mutual interdependence of everything and everybody.

Let me tell you a story about mutual interdependence: Joanna Macy and I happened to be in Australia at the same time several years ago. It was arranged that we should address a group in the Friends Meeting House in Sydney together. I said during my talk that I would like to propose "mutual intersupport" as a new term for "mutual interdependence." It's more active somehow. Joanna heard me say "mutual intersport." She thought that was a great idea. [Laughter] It *is* a great idea and a spin that brings even more vitality to the Buddha's notion of harmony.

Anyway, the third meaning of *Dharma* is "phenomena." This is the Nirmānakāya, the precious nature of each individual thing, being, particle. The old teachers traced some forty other meanings of *Dharma*, so it is a richly ambiguous word. Just translating it as "teaching" takes all the vitality out of the original.

Q. In Zen Buddhism I hear a lot of emphasis on the "don't-know mind." What is the relationship between the "don't-know mind" and knowledge?

R. Bodhidharma knew he didn't know:

> *The Emperor Wu of Liang asked Bodhidharma, "What is the first principle of the holy teaching?"*
>
> *Bodhidharma said, "Vast emptiness, nothing holy."*
>
> *The Emperor asked, "Who is this standing here before me?"*
>
> *Bodhidharma said, "I don't know."*

He leaves and goes on to Western China where a few sincere disciples find him. His religious advisor asks the Emperor if he knows who Bodhidharma really is. The Emperor replies, "I don't know." Yuan-wu, editor of *The Blue Cliff Record*, asks rhetorically, "Is the Emperor's 'I don't know' the same as Bodhidharma's 'I don't know,' or different?[13] It has to be different, of course, but how? This is a basic point.

There's another story:

Ti-ts'ang asked Fa-yen, "What are you up to these days?"

Fa-yen said, "I am on pilgrimage wherever my feet will carry me."

Ti-ts'ang said, "What do you expect from pilgrimage?"

Fa-yen said, "I don't know."

Ti-ts'ang said, "Not knowing is most intimate."

Ti-ts'ang could say that he didn't know—he knew it. Whatever our practice might be, it is concerned with the mystery. Bodhidharma and Ti-ts'ang configure the mystery. These are mellow, seasoned teachers. You too can say "I don't know" when you have touched the source of their words.

Q. You know, I'm a cowgirl. I don't want to impose the map of Japan or Tibet or any of these places onto who I am. I think you know the question here.

R. Believe me, I do! Shall we recite the *Heart Sūtra* in Sino-Japanese or in English? We do both. Shall we do the *Emmei Jikku Kannon Gyō* in Sino-Japanese or in English? We do it in Sino-Japanese and the translation is there in the text.

This is a religion from Asia, you know. I encourage you to buckle down and take in the minimal number of archetypal terms and phrases and personages that convey it. It's all summed up by that term "Buddha Dharma." I'm not saying "the teaching of the truth," because the Buddha Dharma is not the teaching of the truth. At the same time I must respect relevance and Western tradition and so I want to incorporate such words, such powerful words as *nobility* and *decency* into my teaching. It's a tough one.

Q. I have another tough one. This is very hard to say. I want to make a confession that a couple of years ago I decided that I would do tax resistance. I even wrote this wonderful letter on tax resistance that was published in *Fellowship*. I wrote a letter to my guru about it. Every once and a while I tell him what I'm up to and he never gives me advice unless I ask for it. But this time he said to me, "I think it would take too much of your energy right now." I wanted to go back and say that when I made the decision to do it, I felt so wonderful. Everything was coming together and this was just the right thing to do. But then I realized that there was a part of me that was a little bit relieved by his words, because I was also scared. I was also quite puzzled and I wasn't sure how to respond to him. I really struggled with it and what came to me after a while was that it was very good for me not to be so sure that I was doing the right thing. I think that when we're talking about "not knowing" this is maybe in the same category.

R. Well, similar anyway. I felt a certain amount of doubt about my own tax resistance and so did my wife, Anne. It finally led to our giving it up after six or seven years.

Q. I'm not sure if there's a question here but I felt the need to say something before. You were talking about words being teachers and the more precise we are the clearer we are. In the Christian tradition the key word for human interaction is *love.* In the Buddhist tradition it is *Dāna,* but in the Jewish tradition it is *justice.* You alluded to Western tradition and I felt the need to be a voice saying that there's more than one Western tradition.

R. Oh, there certainly is. Moreover, there is nobody more concerned about accuracy and truth in words than the student of Jewish religion.

Q. To get back to a previous point—would you say something about the danger of people just getting lost in words and becoming dictionaries of Asian concepts? Buddhism had been there in China for five hundred years before Bodhidharma appeared. We honor many of those early teachers for their translations but it was Bodhidharma who brought the Mind Seal.

R. That's right. Bodhidharma illuminated the work of Kumārajīva, no doubt. I'm interested in the wisdom of words and not the game of words. I'm always reminding myself about this.

Q. Rōshi, I was very interested in your discussion of archetypes. I'm Irish and Polish and come out of a Catholic background. Now that I'm learning about Avalokiteshvara and Mañjushrī and other Bodhisattvas, I'm starting to have more thoughts about the archetype of the sacred king or queen. There's a book that's big in the men's movement now called *King, Warrior, Magician, Lover* that discusses these four different archetypes people need to become mature. Now when I chant the *Heart Sūtra*, I'm really praying for Avalokita to come and help us.

R. There are different ways of understanding the Bodhisattva. I have told the story of Elsie Mitchell asking Nakagawa Sōen Rōshi, "Is it true that there are heavenly Bodhisattvas?" He said, "Of course there are Bodhisattvas and angels living up in the sky." This might seem to be quite an un-Zen-like response. But really, the long *Kuan-yin Sūtra* is taken up entirely with Kuan-yin's power to save people who call her name. This sūtra takes twenty minutes to recite and is recited every day of the year in every Zen monastery in Japan. There she is on our altar.

Even within a single tradition like Zen Buddhism, there are many different levels of understanding and faith. I remember how surprised I was one day in the bath at Ryūtaku-ji, the temple where I trained more than forty years ago. I was with a group of monks, including a venerable visitor from another monastery. As he sank into the hot water, he murmured aloud, "*Namandabu, Namandabu, Namandabu.*" This is the mantra of the Pure Land Buddhist, *Namu Amida Butsu*—a supplication to Amitābha Buddha as a savior. One would hardly expect to hear this from the lips of an old-time Zen monk.

The Zen Buddhist student in me wants to include this venerable cleric in my intimate Sangha, but the teacher in me asks that he and you, too, take another step. So long as Kuan-yin is up in the sky, she bears responsibility for your conduct, speech, and thought. I want you to bring her down to your own cushions, to your own desk, to your own sink, to your own response. The Jñāna Pāramitā is the perfection of this process. Like Kuan-yin herself, it disappears in the dance with your friends, but sūtras are the music of the dance and their powerful words are the lyrics of the music.

NOTES

Introduction

1. With the rise of the Mahāyāna, Buddhism underwent a schism that left a Southern branch of teachers loyal to the teaching of the Buddha Shākyamuni and a Northern branch of reformers who enlarged upon the original doctrine. The reformed Buddhists called themselves *Mahāyāna,* "Great Vehicle," and called the Southern Buddhists *Hīnayāna,* or "Small Vehicle." No accurate term that is at the same time decent and generous has emerged for the first teaching. It is sometimes called Theravāda, but that is misleading, for Theravāda is simply one sect of many that emerged after the Buddha's time—the one that eventually supplanted the others. Therefore, tentatively and provisionally, I am using the expression *Classical Buddhism* for the teaching of the Buddha and his immediate successors and *Theravāda Buddhism* for the continuation of that teaching after the rise of the Mahāyāna.

The Pāramitās can be found discussed in Har Dayal, **The Bodhisattva Doctrine in Sanskrit Literature** (Delhi: Motilal Banarsidass, 1934), pp. 165–269; Richard A. Gard, **Buddhism** (New York: George Braziller, 1962), pp. 145–50; Akira Hirakawa, **A History of Indian Buddhism: From Shākyamuni to Early Mahāyāna,** trans. by Paul Groner (Honolulu: University of Hawaii Press, 1990), pp. 297–300; and Wm. Theodore De Bary et al., eds., **The Buddhist Tradition in India, China, and Japan** (New York: Random House, 1972), pp. 83–85.

2. De Bary, et al., **The Buddhist Tradition in India, China, and Japan,** pp. 83–84.
3. Dōgen Kigen, "Bendōwa," **Shōbōgenzō.** Cited by Hee-Jin Kim, **Dōgen Kigen: Mystical Realist** (Tucson: University of Arizona Press, 1987), p. 51.
4. Dōgen Kigen, *Genjō-kōan,* **Shōbōgenzō.** Cf. Kazuaki Tanahashi, **Moon in a Dewdrop: Writings of Zen Master Dōgen** (San Francisco: North Point Press, 1985), p. 70.

1. Giving
The Dāna Pāramitā

1. Lewis Hyde, **The Gift: Imagination and the Erotic Life of Property** (New York: Vintage, 1983), p. 11.
2. Ralph Waldo Emerson, "Nature." Emerson, **Nature** [and] Henry David Thoreau, **Walking** (Boston: Beacon Press, 1991), p. 11.
3. Hyde, **The Gift,** p. 28.
4. John Blofeld, trans., **The Zen Teaching of Instantaneous Awakening: Being the Teaching of the Zen Master Hui Hai, Known as the Great Pearl** (Leicester: Buddhist Publishing Group, 1987), pp. 25–26.
5. Ibid., p. 27.
6. Robert Aitken, **The Gateless Barrier: The Wu-men kuan (Mumonkan)** (San Francisco: North Point Press, 1990), p. 279.
7. Cf. Thomas Cleary and J. C. Cleary, **The Blue Cliff Record** (Boston: Shambhala, 1992), p. 66. Also, Robert Aitken, **The Mind of Clover: Essays in Zen Buddhist Ethics** (San Francisco: North Point Press, 1984), p. 71.
8. Aitken, **The Gateless Barrier,** p. 101.
9. Ruth Fuller Sasaki, trans., **The Recorded Sayings of Ch'an Master Lin-chi Hui-chao of Chen Prefecture** (Kyoto: The Institute for Zen Studies, 1975), p. 3.
10. Thomas Cleary, **Shōbōgenzō: Zen Essays by Dōgen** (Honolulu: University of Hawai'i Press, 1986), pp. 117–18.
11. Some commentators reject "within the mind" as superfluous, though I do not. See Philip B. Yampolsky, **The Platform Sutra of the Sixth Patriarch: The Text of the Tun-huang Manuscript** (New

York: Columbia University Press, 1967), p. 143, fn. 96. See Chapter 8 for the Pranidhāna Pāramitā, the Perfection of Aspiration.

12. See the introduction and the quotation from Dōgen Kigen's *Genjō-kōan*, **Shōbōgenzō.**

13. *Hō* is a causative/stimulative marker, and *'ano* is "seed." "Making the seed" would be the literal meaning. *'Ano* also implies secret or hidden knowledge. It is nurtured privately and passed on only when someone is ready to receive it. Kristin Zambucka, **Ano Ano: The Seed** (Honolulu: Mana Publishing Co., 1978), n.p.

14. R. H. Blyth, **Zen in English Literature and Oriental Classics** (Tokyo: Hokuseido Press, 1942).

2. Morality
The Shīla Pāramitā

1. For a history of the precepts, see Har Dayal, **The Bodhisattva Doctrine in Sanskrit Literature** (Delhi: Motilal Banarsidass, 1934), pp. 197–98. See also Robert Aitken, **The Mind of Clover: Essays in Zen Buddhist Ethics** (San Francisco: North Point Press, 1984), pp. 3–119.
2. Cf. Thomas Cleary and J. C. Cleary, **The Blue Cliff Record** (Boston: Shambhala, 1992), p. 432.
3. Robert Aitken, **Encouraging Words: Zen Buddhist Teachings for Western Students** (New York and San Francisco: Pantheon Books, 1993), pp. 189–91.

3. Forbearance
The Kshānti Pāramitā

1. *Bodhisattva Bhūmi*, cited by Har Dayal, **The Bodhisattva Doctrine in Sanskrit Literature** (Delhi: Motilal Banarsidass, 1934), p. 220.
2. Cf. Thomas Cleary, **Book of Serenity** (Hudson, N.Y.: Lindisfarne Press, 1990), p. 268.
3. Ibid., p. 86.

4. Robert Aitken, **A Zen Wave: Bashō's Haiku and Zen** (New York: Weatherhill, 1978), p. 35. See also, R. H. Blyth, **Haiku,** 4 vols. (Tokyo: Hokuseido Press, 1949–52), III: p. 194.
5. Blyth, **Haiku,** III: pp. 195–96.
6. Ibid., p. 192.
7. Ibid.
8. Cf. Thomas Cleary and J. C. Cleary, **The Blue Cliff Record** (Boston: Shambhala, 1992), p. 110.
9. Robert Aitken, **The Gateless Barrier: The Wu-men kuan (Mumonkan)** (San Francisco: North Point Press, 1990), p. 9.
10. D. T. Suzuki, **Manual of Zen Buddhism** (New York: Grove Press, 1960), p. 94.
11. D. T. Suzuki, **Essays in Zen Buddhism: Second Series** (New York: Samuel Weiser, 1970), plate opposite p. 80.
12. Sonja Arntzen, trans., **Ikkyū and the Crazy Cloud Anthology: A Zen Poet of Medieval Japan** (Tokyo: University of Tokyo Press, 1986), p. 119.
13. Suzuki, **Essays in Zen Buddhism: Second Series,** p. 80. Compare Blake, "There Is No Natural Religion," which champions poetry and prophetic vision rather than asceticism. Geoffrey Keynes, **The Complete Writings of William Blake: With Variant Readings** (New York: Oxford University Press, 1972), p. 92.
14. Suzuki, **Manual of Zen Buddhism,** Plate XI.
15. Arthur Braverman, **Mud and Water: A Collection of Talks by the Zen Master Bassui** (San Francisco: North Point Press, 1989), pp. 102–4.
16. Cf. Kazuaki Tanahashi, **Moon in a Dewdrop: Writings of Zen Master Dōgen** (San Francisco: North Point Press, 1985), p. 69.
17. Nicholas Herman [Brother Lawrence], **The Practice of the Presence of God** (Springfield, Pa.: Whitaker House, 1982).
18. *Mu* is commonly the first kōan of Zen Buddhist practice. Aitken, **The Gateless Barrier,** pp. 7–18.
19. Flora Courtois, **An Experience of Enlightenment** (Wheaton, Ill.: Theosophical Press, 1986).
20. The questioner was condensing this story: "A woman came to Hakuin Ekaku Zenji and said, 'Mountains, rivers, and trees are all luminous. How marvelous! How marvelous!' Hakuin said, 'How about the shit in the toilet?' The woman said, 'Don't you know about that, Rōshi?' " I heard this story from Nakagawa Sōen Rōshi. See Kazuaki Tanahashi, **Penetrating Laughter: Hakuin's Zen and**

Art (Woodstock, N.Y.: The Overlook Press, 1984), p. 15, for a different rendering.

21. Watanabe Tameyoshi, **Hakuin Oshō Yuibokushū** (Tokyo: Minyūsha, 1914), n.p. See also Tanahashi, **Penetrating Laughter,** p. 100, for Hakuin's painting of Ikkyū dangling a skull by a length of twine at a New Year celebration.

22. Cf. Blyth, **Haiku,** IV: p. 290.

4. Zeal
The Vīrya Pāramitā

1. Cf. Thomas Cleary and J. C. Cleary, **The Blue Cliff Record** (Boston: Shambhala, 1992), p. 365. See also Robert Aitken, **The Gateless Barrier: The Wu-men kuan (Mumonkan)** (San Francisco: North Point Press, 1990), pp. 130, 281; Robert Aitken, **The Mind of Clover: Essays in Zen Buddhist Ethics** (San Francisco: North Point Press, 1984), p. 94.

2. Flora Courtois, **An Experience of Enlightenment** (Wheaton, Ill.: Theosophical Press, 1986), pp. 20–43.

3. Har Dayal, **The Bodhisattva Doctrine in Sanskrit Literature** (Delhi: Motilal Banarsidass, 1934), pp. 217–20.

4. Thich Nhat Hanh, **Old Path White Cloud** (Berkeley: Parallax Press, 1991), pp. 298–304.

5. Philip Kapleau, **The Three Pillars of Zen: Practice, Teaching, and Enlightenment** (Boston: Beacon Press, 1965), p. 28.

6. Eugene T. Gendlin, **Focusing** (New York: Everest House, 1978).

7. Daisetz Teitaro Suzuki, **The Training of the Zen Buddhist Monk** (Kyoto: The Eastern Buddhist Society, 1934), Plate 35.

8. The Four Noble Abodes are Loving-Kindness, Compassion, Joy in the Liberation of Others, and Equanimity or Impartiality. See Chapter 5.

5. Settled, Focused Meditation
The Dhyāna Pāramitā

1. D. T. Suzuki, **Essays in Zen Buddhism: First Series** (York Beach, Maine: Samuel Weiser, 1985), p. 82.
2. Koken Murano, **Buddha and His Disciples** (Tokyo: Sanyusha, 1932), pp. vii–viii. See also Robert Aitken, **Encouraging Words: Zen Buddhist Teachings for Western Students** (New York and San Francisco: Pantheon Books, 1993), p. 9.
3. Shunryū Suzuki, **Zen Mind, Beginner's Mind** (New York: Weatherhill, 1970), p. 25.
4. Robert Aitken, **The Gateless Barrier: The Wu-men kuan (Mumonkan)** (San Francisco: North Point Press, 1990), p. 255.
5. Cf. Thomas Cleary and J. C. Cleary, **The Blue Cliff Record** (Boston: Shambhala, 1992), p. 510.
6. Cf. ibid.
7. Cf. ibid., p. 386.
8. Cf. Thomas Cleary, **Book of Serenity** (Hudson, N.Y.: Lindisfarne Press, 1990), p. 183.
9. Cf. Yoel Hoffman, **Radical Zen: The Sayings of Jōshū** (Brookline, Mass.: Autumn Press, 1979), p. 77.
10. Cleary and Cleary, **The Blue Cliff Record,** p. 229.
11. Aitken, **The Gateless Barrier,** p. 190.
12. Hee-Jin Kim, **Dōgen Kigen: Mystical Realist** (Tucson: University of Arizona Press, 1987), p. 65.
13. Ibid.
14. Har Dayal, **The Bodhisattva Doctrine in Sanskrit Literature** (Delhi: Motilal Banarsidass, 1934), pp. 225–29.
15. "Song of Zazen." Aitken, **Encouraging Words,** p. 179. The *Nembutsu* is the mantra *Namu Amida Butsu,* "Veneration to Amitābha Buddha." See Chapter 8.
16. The *Lalita-vistara.* Dayal, **The Bodhisattva Doctrine in Sanskrit Literature,** p. 223.
17. Cf. Cleary and Cleary, **The Blue Cliff Record,** p. 290.
18. Hoffman, **Radical Zen,** p. 22.
19. Aitken, **Encouraging Words,** p. 178.
20. David J. Kalupahana, **Principles of Buddhist Psychology** (Albany: State University of New York, 1987).

6. Wisdom
The Prajñā Pāramitā

1. Wong Mou-lam, *The Sūtra of Hui Neng* in **The Diamond Sūtra and the Sūtra of Hui Neng** (Berkeley: Shambhala, 1969), p. 13.
2. Ibid., pp. 27–38.
3. Thomas Cleary, **Book of Serenity** (Hudson, N.Y.: Lindisfarne Press, 1990), p. 104.
4. Ibid., p. 248.
5. Cf. Thomas Cleary and J. C. Cleary, **The Blue Cliff Record** (Boston: Shambhala, 1992), p. 139.
6. Kazuaki Tanahashi, **Moon in a Dewdrop: Writings of Zen Master Dōgen** (San Francisco: North Point Press, 1985), pp. 144, 158–59.
7. Yūhō Yokoi, **Shōbōgenzō** (Tokyo: Sankibō Buddhist Bookstore, 1986), pp. 7–12.
8. Cf. ibid., p. 70.
9. Robert Aitken, **The Gateless Barrier: The Wu-men kuan (Mumonkan)** (San Francisco: North Point Press, 1990), p. 157. Cf. Cleary, **Book of Serenity,** p. 422.
10. Cleary and Cleary, **The Blue Cliff Record,** p. 1.
11. Aitken, **The Gateless Barrier,** p. 157. Cf. Cleary, **Book of Serenity,** p. 422.
12. Bunnō Katō et al., eds. **The Three-Fold Lotus Sūtra: Innumerable Meanings, The Lotus Flower of the Wonderful Law, and Meditation on the Bodhisattva Universal Virtue** (Tokyo: Kōsei Publishing Co., 1987), pp. 319–27.
13. Norman Waddell, trans., **Hakuin's Poison Words for the Heart** (Kyoto: Boroan Press, 1980), p. 12.
14. From a poem by Wu-men. Aitken, **The Gateless Barrier**, p. 226.
15. Cf. Thomas Cleary, **Transmission of Light** (San Francisco: North Point Press, 1990), p. 32.
16. David J. Kalupahana, **Principles of Buddhist Psychology** (Albany: State University of New York, 1987), pp. 44, 47.
17. Cleary, **Book of Serenity**, p. 335.
18. Robert Aitken, **Encouraging Words: Zen Buddhist Teachings for Western Students** (New York and San Francisco: Pantheon Books, 1993), p. 167.
19. "The Great Prajñā Pāramitā Heart Sūtra," ibid., p. 175.

20. Cf. Cleary and Cleary, **The Blue Cliff Record**, p. 275.
21. Aitken, **The Gateless Barrier**, pp. 29–30.

7: Compassionate Means
The Upāya Pāramitā

1. Cf. Thomas Cleary, **Book of Serenity** (Hudson, N.Y.: Lindisfarne Press, 1990), p. 276.
2. Cf. ibid., p. 241.
3. From a Diamond Sangha sūtra dedication. Robert Aitken, **Encouraging Words: Zen Buddhist Teachings for Western Students** (New York and San Francisco: Pantheon Books, 1993), p. 182.
4. Cf. Thomas Cleary and J. C. Cleary, **The Blue Cliff Record** (Boston: Shambhala, 1992), p. 59.
5. The third line of Great Vows for All, the Bodhisattva Vows recited in each Zen Buddhist service. See Chapter 8.
6. Cf. Cleary and Cleary, **The Blue Cliff Record,** p. 408.
7. Cf. ibid.
8. Cf. ibid., p. 511.
9. Cf. ibid., p. 408.
10. Cf. ibid., p. 194.
11. Robert Aitken, **A Zen Wave: Bashō's Haiku and Zen** (New York: Weatherhill, 1978), p. 71. Cf. Cleary and Cleary, **The Blue Cliff Record,** p. 37.
12. Cf. Cleary and Cleary, **The Blue Cliff Record,** p. 437.
13. Charles Bell, **The Religion of Tibet** (Oxford: The Clarendon Press, 1931), p. 140.
14. Cf. ibid., p. 305.
15. Isshū Miura and Ruth Fuller Sasaki, **Zen Dust: The History of the Kōan and Kōan Study in Rinzai (Lin-chi) Zen** (New York: Harcourt Brace & World, 1966), p. 275.
16. Philip Kapleau, **The Three Pillars of Zen: Practice, Teaching, and Enlightenment** (Boston: Beacon Press, 1965), pp. 245–50.

8. Aspiration
The Pranidhāna Pāramitā

1. Kazuaki Tanahashi, **Moon in a Dewdrop: Writings of Zen Master Dōgen** (San Francisco: North Point Press, 1985), p. 31.
2. Har Dayal, **The Bodhisattva Doctrine in Sanskrit Literature** (Delhi: Motilal Banarsidass, 1934), p. 65.
3. D. T. Suzuki, **A Miscellany on the Shin Teachings of Buddhism** (Kyoto: Shinshu Otaniha Shimusho, 1949), p. 13 ff.
4. Heng Ching et al., trans., **Sūtra of the Past Vows of Earth Store Bodhisattva** (New York: Buddhist Text Translation Society, Institute for the Advanced Study of World Religions, 1974), p. 20.
5. Bunnō Katō et al., eds., **The Three-Fold Lotus Sūtra: Innumerable Meanings, The Lotus Flower of the Wonderful Law and Meditation on the Bodhisattva Universal Virtue** (Tokyo: Kōsei Publishing Co., 1987), pp. 304–5.
6. D. T. Suzuki, **Manual of Zen Buddhism** (New York: Grove Press, 1960), p. 36.
7. Robert Aitken, **Encouraging Words: Zen Buddhist Teachings for Western Students** (New York and San Francisco: Pantheon Books, 1993), p. 172.
8. Isshū Miura and Ruth Fuller Sasaki, **Zen Dust: The History of the Kōan and Kōan Study in Rinzai (Lin-chi) Zen** (New York: Harcourt Brace & World, 1966), p. 228.
9. Thomas Cleary, trans., **The Flower Ornament Scripture**, 3 vols. (Boulder: Shambhala, 1984–87), I: pp. 312–23.
10. Ibid., p. 313.
11. Robert Aitken, **The Dragon Who Never Sleeps: Verses for Zen Buddhist Practice** (Monterey, Ky.: Larkspur Press, 1990), p. 52. This book was republished by Parallax Press, Berkeley, Calif., 1992.
12. Cleary, **The Flower Ornament Scripture**, I: pp. 312–29.
13. Dennis Tedlock and Barbara Tedlock, **Teachings from the American Earth: Indian Religion and Philosophy** (New York: Liveright, 1975), p. 21.
14. *Hamlet* I, iii, 116.
15. Eccl. 5:5.
16. Tanahashi, **Moon in a Dewdrop**, p. 33.
17. Robert Aitken, **The Gateless Barrier: The Wu-men kuan (Mumonkan)** (San Francisco: North Point Press, 1990), p. 70.

18. Thich Nhat Hanh, **Present Moment, Wonderful Moment: Mindfulness Verses for Daily Living** (Berkeley: Parallax Press, 1990). See also notes 9–11.
19. Tanahashi, **Moon in a Dewdrop**, p. 34.
20. Ibid., p. 35.
21. The first few words of the **Heart Sūtra.** See Aitken, **Encouraging Words**, p. 173.

9. Spiritual Power
The Bala Pāramitā

1. Har Dayal, **The Bodhisattva Doctrine in Sanskrit Literature** (Delhi: Motilal Banarsidass, 1934), p. 141.
2. Soothill and Hodous, **A Dictionary of Chinese Buddhist Terms,** p. 46.
3. See Chapter 7.
4. Robert Aitken, **The Mind of Clover: Essays in Zen Buddhist Ethics** (San Francisco: North Point Press, 1984), p. 52.
5. Cf. Thomas Cleary, **Transmission of Light** (San Francisco: North Point Press, 1990), p. 114.
6. Cf. Thomas Cleary and J. C. Cleary, **The Blue Cliff Record** (Boston: Shambhala, 1992), p. 164.
7. Cf. ibid., p. 341.
8. Cf. ibid., p. 10.
9. D. T. Suzuki, **Manual of Zen Buddhism** (New York: Grove Press, 1960), p. 76.
10. Robert Aitken, **Encouraging Words: Zen Buddhist Teachings for Western Students** (New York and San Francisco: Pantheon Books, 1993), p. 186.
11. Cf. ibid., pp. 279–80.
12. Part of the evening message at the end of sesshin. Aitken, **Encouraging Words,** p. 183.
13. Quoted by Lewis Hyde, **The Gift: Imagination and the Erotic Life of Property** (New York: Vintage, 1983), p. 17. See also his chapter, "A Draft of Whitman," p. 160 ff.
14. Yoel Hoffman, **Radical Zen: The Sayings of Joshū** (Brookline, Mass.: Autumn Press, 1979), p. 30.

15. Robert Aitken, **The Gateless Barrier: The Wu-men kuan (Mumonkan)** (San Francisco: North Point Press, 1990), p. 19.
16. See Chapter 1.
17. A reference to Case 38 of the *Wu-men kuan*. Aitken, **The Gateless Barrier**, p. 231.
18. James Stephens et al., **English Romantic Poets** (New York: American Book Co., 1935), p. 712.

10. Knowledge
The Jñāna Pāramitā

1. See Chapter 7.
2. Robert Aitken, **Taking the Path of Zen** (San Francisco: North Point Press, 1982), pp. 115–32.
3. See Chapter 8.
4. Unpublished letter from Susan Garfield, a psychotherapist living in Oakland, California, August 21, 1992.
5. See Chapter 2.
6. Cited by Hee-Jin Kim, "The Reason of Words and Letters: Dōgen and Kōan Language," in William LaFleur, ed., **Dōgen Studies** (Honolulu: University of Hawai'i Press, 1985), p. 57.
7. Robert Aitken, **The Gateless Barrier: The Wu-men kuan (Mumonkan)** (San Francisco: North Point Press, 1990), p. 174. Cf. Thomas Cleary and J. C. Cleary, **The Blue Cliff Record** (Boston: Shambhala, 1992), p. 211.
8. Cited by R. H. Blyth, **Zen in English Literature and Oriental Classics** (New York: Dutton, 1960), p. 44.
9. Ibid., p. 224.
10. Cf. Cleary and Cleary, **The Blue Cliff Record,** p. 226.
11. Susanne K. Langer, **Philosophy in a New Key: A Study in the Symbolism of Reason, Rite, and Art** (Cambridge, Mass.: Harvard University Press, 1957).
12. Cf. Cleary and Cleary, **The Blue Cliff Record**, p. 472.
13. Cf. ibid., pp. 1–4.

GLOSSARY

Japanese names are given in the traditional order, with surnames first. For Mahāyāna, read Mahāyāna Buddhist or Buddhism. For Zen, read Zen Buddhist or Buddhism. For Rinzai or Sōtō, read Rinzai or Sōtō Zen Buddhist or Buddhism. Note that Sanskrit terms that conventionally begin with Ś will be found under *Sh*. Abbreviations: c=century; C=Chinese; J=Japanese; P=Pali; S=Sanskrit.

Ahimsā, S. Nonharming, nurturing.

Amitābha, S. Amida. The Buddha of Infinite Light and Life who saves sentient beings and presides over the Pure Land.

Ānanda, 4th c., B.C.E. One of the principal disciples of the Buddha **Shākyamuni;** the second Ancestral Teacher.

Anuttara-samyaksambodhi, S. Supreme perfect enlightenment. Total unitive fulfillment.

Avalokiteshvara, S. Sovereign Observer. Archetypal Bodhisattva of mercy. *See* **Kanzeon.**

Bankei Yōtaku (Zenji), 1622–1693. Japanese Rinzai master noted for his capacity to communicate with lay students.

Bassui Tokushō (Zenji), 1327–1378. Japanese Rinzai master noted for his appeal to the Bodhichitta in his disciples.

Blue Cliff Record, The, Pi-yen-lu, C. ***Hekigan-roku,*** J. A collection of 100 cases used for Zen study, usually associated with the Rinzai school, with commentaries by Yüan-wu K'o-ch'in (1063–1135).[1]

Bodhichitta, S. The aspiration for enlightenment and Buddhahood.

Bodhidharma (6th c.) Semi-legendary Indian or West Asian founder of Ch'an Buddhism; archetype for steadfast practice.

Bodhisattva, S. One on the path to enlightenment; one who is enlightened; one who enlightens others; a figure in the Buddhist pantheon.

Bodhi tree. *Ficus religiosa.* The tree that sheltered the Buddha Shākyamuni before, during, and just after his realization.

Book of Serenity, Ts'ung-jung-lu, C. *Shōyō-roku,* J. A collection of 100 cases used for Zen study, usually associated with the Sōtō school, with commentaries by Hung-chih Cheng-chueh, 1091–1157.[2]

Brahma-vihāra, S. Sublime or Noble Abode. The four progressive Brahma-vihāras are Maitrī, boundless loving-kindness; Karunā, boundless compassion; Muditā, boundless joy in the liberation of others; and Upekshā, boundless equanimity.

Buddha Tao *or* **Way.** Buddha Dharma. The Eightfold Path.

Buddhist Peace Fellowship. A network of autonomous groups of Buddhists concerned about peace, social justice, and the protection of all beings, with a communications center in Berkeley, California.

Ch'an, C. Zen.

Chao-chou Ts'ung-shen, 778–897. Jōshū Jūshin, J. An especially revered Chinese Ch'an master.

Cheng-tao ke, C; *Shōdōka,* J; *Song of Realizing the Way.* A long Dharma poem by Yung-chia Hsüan-chüeh, 665–713.[3]

Codependent arising. Mutual interdependence.

Dharma, S. Religious, secular, or natural law; the law of karma; Buddha Dharma or Tao; teaching; the Dharmakāya.

---

[1]Thomas Cleary and J. C. Cleary, *The Blue Cliff Record* (Boston: Shambhala, 1992).

[2]Thomas Cleary, *Book of Serenity* (Hudson, N.Y.: Lindisfarne Press, 1990).

[3]Sheng-yen, *The Sword of Wisdom: Lectures on "The Song of Enlightenment"* (Elmhurst, N.Y.: Dharma Drum Publications, 1990).

Dharmakāya, S. *See* **Three Bodies (of the Buddha).**

Dharma encounter. A ceremony of public question and response with the rōshi.

Dharma successor. One who has received transmission from an authentic master.

Dharma Wheel. The evolution of the Buddha Dharma in universal consciousness.

Dhyāna, S. Focused meditation and its form. Zazen, Zen. *See* **Samādhi.**

Diamond Sangha. A network of Zen centers originally founded in Honolulu in the Sanbō Kyōdan line.

Dōgen Kigen, 1200–1253. Venerated as the Japanese founder of the Sōtō tradition.

Dōjō, J. Bodhimanda. The training hall or zendō. One's own place of realization. The seat of the Buddha beneath the Bodhi tree.

Dokusan, J. Sanzen. To work alone; personal interview with the rōshi during formal practice.

Duhkha, S. Anguish; a response to mortality and dependence. The consequences of denying that reality. The first of the Four Noble Truths.

Eightfold Path. The ideals and practice of right views, right thoughts, right speech, right conduct, right livelihood, right effort or lifestyle, right recollection, and right meditation (in keeping with the insubstantial nature of the self, mutual interdependence, and the sacred nature of each being). The way of freeing oneself from Duhkha. The fourth of the Four Noble Truths.

Emmei Jikku Kannon Gyō, J. "Ten-Verse Kannon Sūtra of Timeless Life."[4]

Engaku Monastery. Rinzai monastery in Kamakura, Japan.

Four Noble Abodes. Brahma Vihāras.

Four Noble Truths. Anguish is everywhere; there is a cause of anguish; there is liberation from anguish; liberation is the Eightfold Path. The basic Buddhist teaching.

---

[4]Robert Aitken, *Encouraging Words: Zen Buddhist Teachings for Western Students* (New York and San Francisco: Pantheon Books, 1993), p. 178.

Gateless Barrier, The, Wu-men kuan, C; *Mumonkan,* J. Basic collection of forty-eight classic Zen cases used for Zen study, compiled with commentaries by Wu-men Hui-k'ai.[5]

Gāthā, S. A four-line verse that sums up an aspect of the Dharma. In the Mahāyāna it is often a vow.

Hakuin Ekaku (Zenji), 1685–1768. Japanese Rinzai master and artist; ancestor of all contemporary Rinzai teachers.

Harada Dai'un *or* **Sogaku,** 1870–1961. Japanese Zen founder of the Syncretic School that became the Sanbō Kyōdan. Teacher of Yasutani Haku'un and of Westerners.

Heart Sūtra. Prajñāpāramitā-hridaya-sūtra, S; *Hannya Shingyō,* J. A brief summary of the Mahāyāna, stressing the complementarity of substance and emptiness.

Hīnayāna, S. Small Vehicle (pejorative). Schools of Classical or Southern Buddhism, of which only Theravāda survives.

Hsin-hsin ming, C; *Shinjinmei,* J; *Precepts of Faith in Mind.* A long Dharma poem attributed to the Third Chinese Ancestor Seng-ts'an, d. 606.[6]

Hua-yen ching *or* ***Hua-yen Sūtra.*** Chinese version of the *Avatamsaka Sūtra,* which stresses the particularity of all beings and their innate harmony.[7]

Hui-neng, C, 638–713. Sixth Ancestral Teacher. Traditionally the key figure in Ch'an Buddhist acculturation.

Ikkyū Sōjun, 1394–1481. Japanese Rinzai master, poet, renowned for his resolute independence from convention.

Jizō, J; Ti-ts'ang, C; Kshitigarbha, S. Earth treasury or -womb. Archetypal Bodhisattva who saves living and dead children, wayfarers, fishermen, and people in hell. Distinguish from Lo-han Kuei-ch'en, 867–928, a Chinese master who was also known as Ti-ts'ang.

Jukai, J. The ceremony of accepting the Buddha as one's teacher and the Precepts as guides.

---

[5]Robert Aitken, *The Gateless Barrier: The Wu-men kuan (Mumonkan)* (San Francisco: North Point Press, 1990).

[6]Shen-yen, *Faith in Mind: A Guide to Ch'an Practice* (Elmhurst, N.Y.: Dharma Drum Publications, 1987).

[7]Thomas Cleary, trans., *The Flower Ornament Scripture: A Translation of the Avatamsaka Sūtra,* 3 vols. (Boulder: Shambhala, 1984–87).

Kannon, J. Kanzeon, Kuan-yin.

Kanzeon, Kannon, J. Kuan-yin. One who hears the sounds of the world; the archetypal Bodhisattva of mercy. Derived from Avalokiteshvara.

Karma, S. Action. Cause and effect; affinity; the function of mutual interdependence. Distinguish from fate.

Karunā, S. *See* **Brahma-vihāra.**

"Kats'," "Katsu," J. **"Khat,"** C. The shout that wipes clean.

Keizan Jōkin, 1268–1325. Japanese great-grandson in the Dharma of Dōgen Kigen, compiler of the *Denkō-roku,* J. (*Transmission of Light*).[8]

Kenshō, J. Seeing (True) Nature. Realization. *See* Satori.

Kesa, J. A robe worn over the usual robe on formal occasions by Mahāyāna monks and nuns, patterned after the traditional single square of cloth worn by the Buddha.

Kinhin, J. Walking verification. Sūtra walk. The formal walk between periods of zazen.

Klesha, S; Bonnō, J. Afflictions, obstacles. The Three Poisons.

Kōan, J. Universal/Particular. A presentation of the harmony of the Universal and the Particular; a theme of zazen to be made clear. A classic mondō, or Zen story.

Koko An, J. The Little Temple Here. Diamond Sangha training center in Honolulu.

Kuan-yin, C. Kannon, Kanzeon.

Kumārajīva, 344–413. Central Asian Buddhist master instrumental in translating important Buddhist texts into Chinese.

Kyosaku *or* **Keisaku,** J. Stick of encouragement carried by a dōjō leader and applied to the shoulders upon request to stimulate concentration.

Lin-chi I-hsüan, d. 866. Venerated as the Chinese founder of the Lin-chi (Rinzai) school.

Lotus of the Subtle Law Sūtra. *Saddharmapundarīka-sūtra,* S. Teachings of the Middle Way in parables.[9]

Mahāyāna, S. Great Vehicle; the Buddhism of East Asia, also

---

[8]Thomas Cleary, *Transmission of Light* (San Francisco: North Point Press, 1990).

[9]Bunnō Katō et al., trans., *The Threefold Lotus Sūtra* (New York: Weatherhill, 1975).

found in Vietnam. Tibetan Buddhism is often considered to be Mahāyāna. The practice of saving the many beings.

Maitreya, S. The Compassionate One; the future, potential, or inherent Buddha.

Mañjushrī, S. Beautiful Virtue; archetypal Bodhisattva of wisdom.

Māra. The Destroyer. The Evil One.

Maui Zendō. A training center of the Diamond Sangha, closed in 1986.

Middle Way. The Way of the Buddha, harmonizing the Particular and the Universal, Cause and Effect, Essential Nature and Phenomena, the Three Bodies of the Buddha. The Eightfold Path.

Mu, J; Wu, C. No; does not have. A kōan from Case 1 of *The Gateless Barrier.*

Mudrā, S. A seal or sign; hand or finger position or gesture that presents an aspect of the Dharma.

Nakagawa Sōen, 1907–1984. Japanese Zen master of Ryūtaku Monastery; teacher of Westerners.

Nembutsu, J. Recalling Buddha. The Pure Land School practice of repeating "Namu Amida Butsu": "Veneration to the Buddha Amitābha."

Nirmānakāya, S. *See* **Three Bodies (of the Buddha).**

Nirodha, S. Extinction, annhilation, cessation, the third of the Four Noble Truths.

Nirvāna, S. Liberation found in practice and realization. *See* **Pure Land.**

Pālolo Zen Center. A training center of the Diamond Sangha in Honolulu.

Pāramitā, S. Perfection as condition or practice. Cross over (to the shore of Nirvāna). Save; transform. The roster of Shīla; the moral code. *See* **Jukai.**

Prajñā, S. Wisdom, enlightenment, realization.

Precepts. The roster of Shīla, the moral code. *See* **Jukai.**

Pure Land. Nirvāna; the afterlife envisioned in the Pure Land schools of Buddhism. Lotus Land. Realized as this very place.

Pu-tai (Hotei, J). The so-called Laughing Buddha, associated with Maitreya. A god of good fortune.

Rebirth. The coherent, changing karma of an individual or a cluster of individuals reappearing after death. The continuous arising of coherent, changing karma during life. Distinguish from **Reincarnation.**

Reincarnation. The notion that an enduring self reappears after death in a new birth. Distinguish from **Rebirth.**

Rinzai Gigen, Japanese for Lin-chi I-hsüan.

Rinzai Zen Buddhism. Today the Zen school in which kōan study is used in conjunction with zazen.

Rōhatsu Sesshin, J. Eight-Day Sesshin in Great Cold, celebrating the enlightenment of the Buddha Shākyamuni, December 8.

Rōshi, J. Old teacher. Now the title of the confirmed Zen teacher.

Ryūtaku Monastery. Zen monastery in Mishima, Japan.

Samādhi, S. Absorption. The quality of zazen. One with the universe. *See* **Dhyāna.**

Samantabhadra, S. Pervading Goodness. Archetypal Bodhisattva of great compassionate action.

Sambhogakāya, S. *See* **Three Bodies (of the Buddha).**

Sanbō Kyōdan. Order of the Three Treasures. A lay Japanese Sōtō tradition that includes elements of Rinzai practice, founded by Yasutani Haku'un in Kamakura, Japan.

Sangha, S. Aggregate. Buddhist community; any community, including that of all beings.

Satori, J. Prajñā, Enlightenment; the condition or (sometimes) the experience of enlightenment. *See* **Kenshō.**

Senzaki, Nyogen, 1876–1958. First Japanese Zen teacher to settle in the West. A disciple of Shaku Sōen Zenji.

Sesshin, J. To touch, receive, and convey the mind. The intensive Zen retreat of three to seven days.

Shaku Sōen (Zenji), 1859–1919. Japanese Master of Engaku Monastery in Kamakura. Teacher of D. T. Suzuki and Nyogen Senzaki.

Shākyamuni, S. Sage of the Shākya Clan; the historical Buddha, 5th–4th c., B.C.E. Founder of Buddhism. Archetype of Prajñā, Karunā, and the Nirmānakāya.

Shāriputra, S. 4th c., B.C.E. A prominent heir of the Buddha Shākyamuni, interlocutor in the *Heart Sūtra.*

Shikan, J. Shamatha/Vipashyanā. The meditation of the Tendai School. *See* **T'ien-t'ai, Shikantaza, Zazen.**

Shikantaza, J. Body and Mind Dropped Away in zazen.

Shīla, S. Restraint. Keeping the precepts.

Shōbō-genzō, J. *True Dharma Eye Treasury.* The collection of Dōgen's many essays on Zen and its practice.

Skandha, S. Aggregate. The five skandhas are forms of the world:

sensation, perception, mental formulation, and consciousness. These make up the self and are realized as empty.

Sōtō Zen Buddhism. Today the Zen school that uses shikantaza as a principal practice in zazen.

Sūtra, S. Sermons by the Buddha Shākyamuni and those attributed to him; Buddhist scripture. *See* **Tripitaka.**

Suzuki Daisetz (D. T. Suzuki), 1870–1966. Japanese lay disciple of Shaku Sōen. The scholar most responsible for the dissemination of knowledge about Zen in the West.

Suzuki Shunryū, 1904–1971. Japanese Sōtō founder and first abbot of the San Francisco Zen Center.

Taking Refuge. The ceremony of acknowledging the Buddha, Dharma, and Sangha as one's home, common to all Buddhist traditions. *See* **Precepts; Jukai.**

Tan, J. Row; line of people doing zazen. Dōjō.

Tao, C. Way. Buddha Dharma; the Eightfold Path. Distinguish from the Tao of Taoism.

Tathāgata, S. One who comes forth (presenting essential nature with particular qualities). A Buddha. Shākyamuni.

Teishō, J. Presentation of the shout; the Dharma presented by the rōshi in a public talk.

Theravāda, S. Way of the Elders. Today the Buddhism of south and Southeast Asia. *See* **Hīnayāna.**

Three Bodies (of the Buddha). The complementary natures of buddhahood and the world: Dharmakāya, the Dharma or law body of essential nature; Sambhogakāya, the bliss body of mutual interdependence; and Nirmānakāya, the transformation body of uniqueness and variety.

Three Poisons. Greed, Hatred, and Ignorance: the main kinds of self-centeredness that hinder the practice. *See* **Klesha.**

Three Treasures or Jewels. The Buddha, Dharma, and Sangha; enlightenment, the Way, and community: the basic elements of Buddhism.

Three Vows of Refuge. *See* **Taking Refuge; Jukai; Precepts.**

T'ien-t'ai, C; Tendai, J. Early school of Chinese Buddhism that includes scholastic, devotional, esoteric, and meditative teachings. An antecedent of subsequent schools.

Tripitaka, S. Three Baskets. The three main teachings of Buddhism: Sūtras, the Vinaya, and the Abhidharma, or Commentaries.

Upāya, S. Skillful, appropriate means in turning the Dharma Wheel, or prompting realization.

Vajrayāna, S. The Way of the Adamantine Truth; Tibetan Buddhism.

Vinaya, S. The moral teachings. *See* **Tripitaka.**

Vipashyanā, S; Vipassanā, P. Insight. The meditative practice of seeing into the insubstantial nature of the self and its sensations, thoughts, and emotions.

Wu-men Hui-K'ai, C; Mumon Ekai, J, 1183–1260. Chinese master, compiler of *The Gateless Barrier.*

Yamada Kōun *or* **Zenshin,** 1907–1989. Japanese master of the Sanbō Kyōdan; teacher of Westerners.

Yamamoto Gempō, 1866–1961. Japanese Rinzai master of Ryūtaku Monastery; teacher of Nakagawa Sōen.

Yasutani Haku'un *or* **Ryōko,** 1895–1973. Japanese founder of the Sanbō Kyōdan; teacher of Yamada Kōun and of Westerners.

Zazen, J. The practice of seated, focused meditation; formal Zen practice. Dhyāna.

Zendō, J. Zen hall; Zen center. **Dōjō.**

Zenji, J. Zen master (posthumous title).

ABOUT THE AUTHOR

Robert Aitken was first introduced to Zen in a Japanese internment camp during World War II. R. H. Blyth, author of *Zen in English Literature and Oriental Classics,* was imprisoned in the same camp, and in this setting Aitken began the first of several apprenticeships. After the war Aitken returned often to Japan to study. He became friends with Daisetz T. Suzuki and studied with Nakagawa Sōen Rōshi and Yasutani Haku'un Rōshi. In 1959 he and his wife, Anne, established the Diamond Sangha, a Zen Buddhist society with headquarters in Hawaii. Aitken was given the title "Rōshi" and was authorized to teach by Yamada Kōun Rōshi in 1974; he received full transmission from Yamada Rōshi in 1985. He continues to write, teach, and practice in Hawaii, where he has lived since the age of five.